137 GUITAR SPEED & COORDINATION EXERCISES

Groundbreaking Guitar Technique Strategies for Synchronization, Speed and Practice

CHRIS BROOKS

FUNDAMENTAL CHANGES

137 Guitar Speed & Coordination Exercises

Groundbreaking Guitar Technique Strategies for Synchronization, Speed and Practice

ISBN: 978-1-78933-398-5

Copyright © 2022 Christopher A. Brooks

Edited by Tim Pettingale

The moral right of this author has been asserted.

All rights reserved. No part of this publication may be reproduced, stored in a retrieval system, or transmitted in any form or by any means, without prior permission in writing from the publisher.

The publisher is not responsible for websites (or their content) that are not owned by the publisher.

www.fundamental-changes.com

Twitter: **@guitar_joseph**

Over 10,000 fans on Facebook: **FundamentalChangesInGuitar**

Facebook: **ChrisBrooksGuitar**

Instagram: **FundamentalChanges**

Instagram: **chrisbrooksguitarist**

For over 350 Free Guitar Lessons with Videos Check Out

www.fundamental-changes.com

Cover Image Copyright: Shutterstock, Tongra Jantaduang

Contents

Introduction 4

Get the Audio and Video 5

Section One: Locking In 6

Chapter One: Improving Your Internal Rhythm 7
    Foot tapping 7
    Synchronized Subdivisions 9

Chapter Two: Single String Synchronization 13
    Chromatic Synchronization Picking Drills 15
    Finger Independence 19
    The twenty-four permutations of 1-2-3-4 20

Chapter Three: Diatonic Cells and Permutations 23
    Synchronized Position Shifts 31

Chapter Four: String Crossing – Alternate Picking 37

Chapter Five: String Crossing – Sweep and Economy Picking 47

Chapter Six: Legato and Picking Interplay 55

Section One Summary 62

Section Two: Speeding Up 63

Chapter Seven: Playing Without Tension 64
    Posture and Position 65
    Fretting Hand Pressure 66
    Picking Hand Attack 70
    Troubleshooting: Wayward Pick Strokes 75

Chapter Eight: The Speed Practice System 77
    Zip files for your mind 78
    Finding your continuous top speed 78
    Application: Single Strings 80
    The chicken and egg of "small movements" 87
    Application: String Changes 88
    Other Speed Practice Strategies 92
    The Science of Modified Practice 95

Chapter Nine: Speed and Endurance Etudes 96

Section Two Summary 102

Conclusion 103

Other Books by Chris Brooks 104

Introduction

Welcome to my book on synchronization and speed for guitar. If you've long searched for the right material to perfect your technique, to get your hands to work together and learn to play faster, I wrote this for you!

Playing the guitar fast highly depends upon both hands being locked into each other. Synchronization is the positive outcome of the picking and fretting hands performing separate tasks as one unit. Beyond a few internet workouts and occasional paragraphs in books, I rarely see this skill addressed in much detail.

With our hands often travelling along different axes – the picking hand working vertically while the fretting hand works horizontally (and vertically, and diagonally!) – it's no wonder that synchronization can be a stumbling block for many players, especially where speed and fluidity are desired.

As creatures of habit, we guitarists can sometimes be guilty of letting a few things slide until they become unwanted habits. An error here or there, baked in with hundreds of hours of practice, can be troublesome to get rid of when we've decided it's time to do better.

Seeing where people still struggle with coordination and synchronization was the impetus for this book. The chapters of Section One aim to tidy up various things that might be holding you back without you even knowing it.

A massive component of synchronization is *timing* – executing commands at the precise moment we intend. This book examines timing in stages, beginning with internal rhythm, then locking the picking hand into the beat, and then locking the fretting hand fingers in with the picking hand.

In chapters four, five, and six, we'll look at ways to improve the synchronization of alternate picking, sweep picking, economy picking, and legato. I won't be teaching these techniques from scratch, so it's assumed you have some playing experience already. If not, it will be highly valuable to check out my other technique methods from Fundamental Changes.

I'll also introduce my LIE (*locate, isolate, exaggerate*) concept for troubleshooting individual problems and addressing them head-on.

In Section Two (*Speeding Up*), we'll tackle *speed development*.

Just as walking doesn't turn into running and sprinting by repetition alone, speed doesn't occur simply by practicing slow and waiting to see what happens. It's time to treat speeding up as an area in itself.

Throughout this section, you'll learn my strategies for playing without tension, creating dynamics with technique instead of muscle strain, and applying a practice system that will make you faster from the very first session.

You won't require superhuman strength to play fast, but you may have to look at things differently, keep an open mind, and try new things. We need to set your playing free to achieve speed, so let's stop waiting for it to happen naturally!

For both sections of the book, it's essential to have a metronome close by. You can use a physical metronome (as used by old-timers like me), desktop apps (even Google has a free metronome) or one of the many apps available in app stores for mobile devices.

Are you ready? Let's lock in and speed up!

Chris Brooks

Get the Audio and Video

The audio files for this book are available to download for free from **www.fundamental-changes.com.** The link is in the top right-hand corner. Simply select this book title from the drop-down menu and follow the instructions to get the audio.

We recommend that you download the files directly to your computer, not to your tablet, and extract them there before adding them to your media library. You can then put them on your tablet, iPod or burn them to CD. On the download page, there is a help PDF, and we also provide technical support via the contact form.

Bonus Video Content

Bonus video content accompanying this book can be found at:

https://geni.us/speedguitar

For over 350 Free Guitar Lessons with Videos Check out:

www.fundamental-changes.com

Twitter: **@guitar_joseph**

Over 10,000 fans on Facebook: **FundamentalChangesInGuitar**

Instagram: **FundamentalChanges**

Section One: Locking In

Timing is everything!

Synchronization for guitarists is often reduced to specific finger-twisting drills or some well-meaning advice about playing slow. Both approaches can be helpful, but neither is holistic.

This section of the book looks at synchronization by exploring inner timing, picking hand timing, and fretting hand timing as individual contributors to the overall goal of playing in sync.

When I talk about timing, I'm not referring to *time feel*, where an experienced player exerts control over playing ahead or behind the beat with purpose. A player who can do that makes a musical choice to create an effect using time.

What we want to do through the chapters ahead is make timing – and therefore synchronization – the operating system that all areas of your technique benefit from. You'll then have more freedom to make musical choices without repeatedly tripping over certain mechanical things in the same spots.

When playing the exercises in this section, do so confidently. Use precise, audible pick strokes and avoid masking any issues by being too meek in your execution. The best way to highlight weaknesses is to shine a light on them.

Let's begin with getting your body in time with the metronome.

Chapter One: Improving Your Internal Rhythm

Synchronizing your left and right hands is a big aim of this book! Before we do that, though, we need to synchronize our bodies with the beat. Even if the hands are in-sync with each other, it's crucial to avoid drifting in and out of time.

You've probably already experienced the feeling of knowing a guitar part (and possibly even playing with synchronized hands) but drifting behind or ahead of the beat of the song when you didn't mean to.

In this chapter, you'll learn to lock into 1/4 note beats using one foot for tapping and your picking hand. Then, we'll use that foundation to execute various rhythmic tasks with the picking hand.

Foot tapping will become your subconscious acknowledgement of the pulse of the music you're playing, and the picking hand will be the engine room of playing your guitar in time.

Foot tapping

If you pick with your right hand, getting used to tapping with your left foot is a good idea. I've always found, as with walking and running, that our limbs maintain good rhythm in opposites. If you play left-handed, try tapping the right foot.

To begin with, keep your heel on the ground and tap with your toes. This gives you a straightforward motion to control for now.

Later, to avoid fatigue and muscle strain, and when playing faster, you can try incorporating the heel with either a *toe-heel-toe-heel* or *heel-toe-heel-toe* motion. Whichever version you choose, keep it alternating and don't double up on toes or heels because you'll throw yourself off! (NB: A heel tap is done with the toes still in contact with the floor).

Example 1a is written in rhythmic notation. This form will be used for the metronome clicks and your foot taps in several examples. Each bar contains four 1/4 notes – the same rhythm your metronome will click at.

Set your metronome to 80 beats per minute (bpm) and tap the foot opposite your picking hand. There's no guitar or pick required yet.

Keep it going until you lock each tap of your foot into each click of the metronome. The slower the tempo, the more challenging the task, because it's easier to come in early or late.

Example 1a:

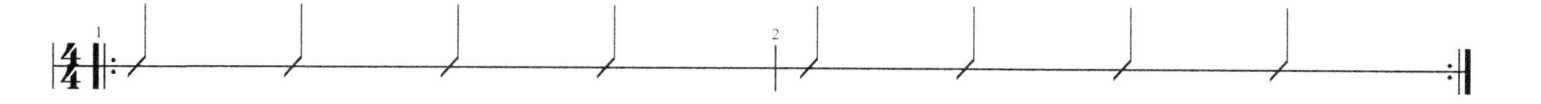

Repeat the above example at 100bpm, 120bpm, 140bpm, and 160bpm. From 120bpm upwards, switch to a *heel-toe* or *toe-heel* tapping motion.

Now, repeat the exercise above but add a slap of your picking hand to your leg (the one that's not foot tapping).

In other words, your foot tap and your picking hand slap should both be in sync with the click. Do this at all the previous speeds.

Now, grab your guitar and a pick as we approach the remaining examples.

Example 1b replaces the hand taps from the previous exercise with notes and downstrokes on the guitar. The guitar part is written in the notation and tablature. The metronome clicks (and foot taps) are written on the bottom line for reference.

There's nothing complicated about playing the same note four times in a bar, but the aim is to lock in with the metronome as close to perfect as possible.

Play this example in 20bpm increments from 80bpm to 160bpm, using foot taps at each tempo.

Example 1b:

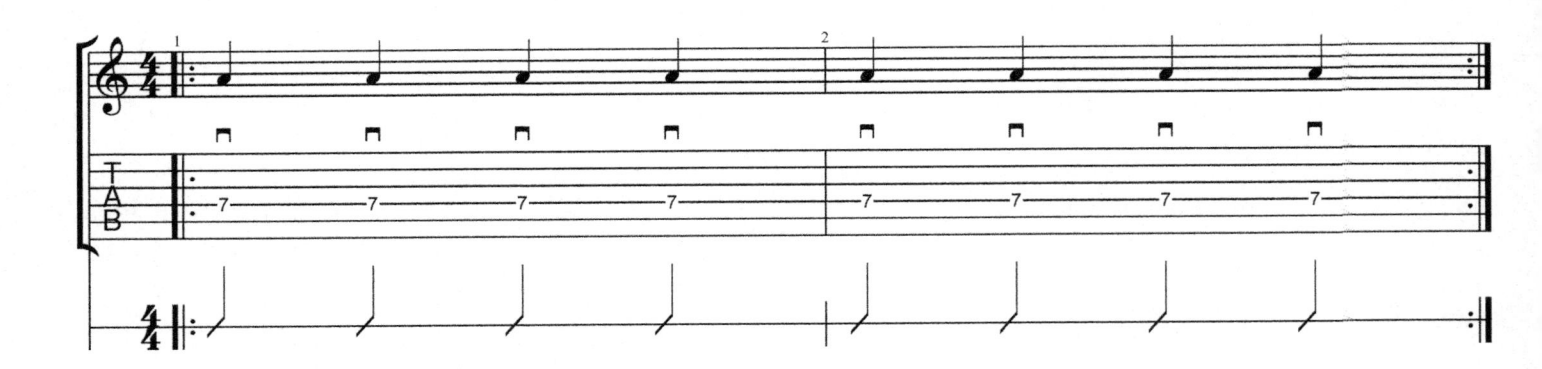

Synchronized Subdivisions

It's time to task the picking hand with some beat subdivisions. The following examples are crucial for independence between your body's left and right sides. In each example, keep the metronome ticking and your foot tapping.

In Example 1c, the metronome and foot are working at 1/4 notes while the guitar plays 1/8th notes, i.e., two notes per beat.

The second picked downstroke of each beat must sound exactly halfway between each 1/4 beat. Begin at a comfortable tempo and accelerate in 10-20bpm increments.

Example 1c:

Alternating pick strokes at slow speeds can be harder to time perfectly than all-downstroke 1/8th notes, so let's modify the previous example and work on that.

An important tip for well-timed alternate picking is to keep the width of the picking motion equal on either side of the string. If the string isn't the centre point of your down/up motion, you risk creating an unintended swing or shuffle when one pick stroke moves further away from the string than the other.

Example 1d:

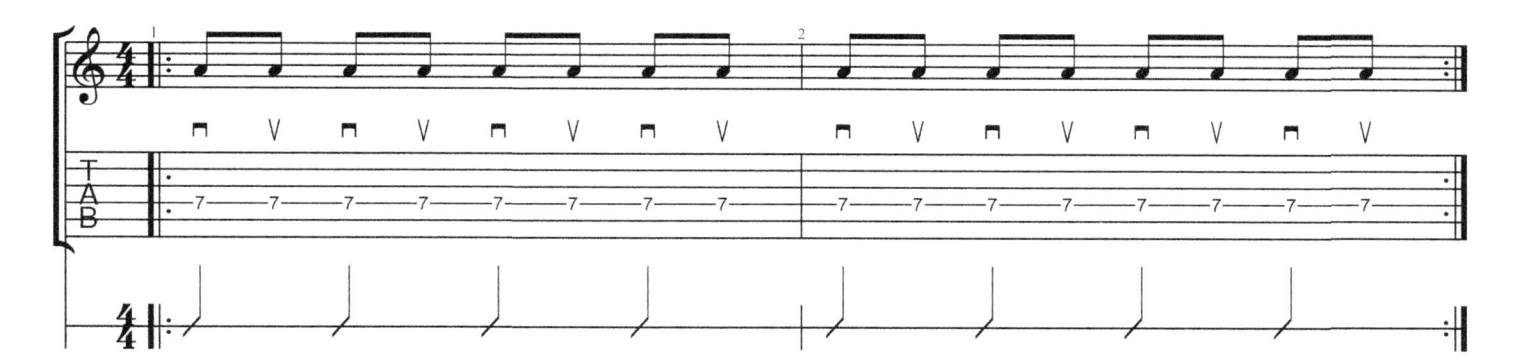

Let's switch between down-picked 1/8th notes and alternate-picked 1/16th notes while maintaining the pulse of the foot and metronome.

For economical 1/16th notes, pick down and up in straight, logical lines of motion, rather than scooping the pick in an out of the strings on every note (see bonus video for a comparison).

Example 1e:

To play 1/8th triplets against 1/4 note foot taps, let's first try them with all downstrokes.

Each set of three notes should be evenly spaced across the beat and into the next beat. Avoid having your triplets sound more like a gallop by counting an evenly spaced *one-and-ah, two-and-ah, three-and-ah, four-and-ah* aloud.

Example 1f:

When alternate picking 1/8th note triplets, you'll begin every second set on an upstroke. Don't let this interrupt the picking timing or your foot taps. If it does, play unaccompanied for a moment, counting the triplets out loud until you can resume playing to the beat.

Example 1g:

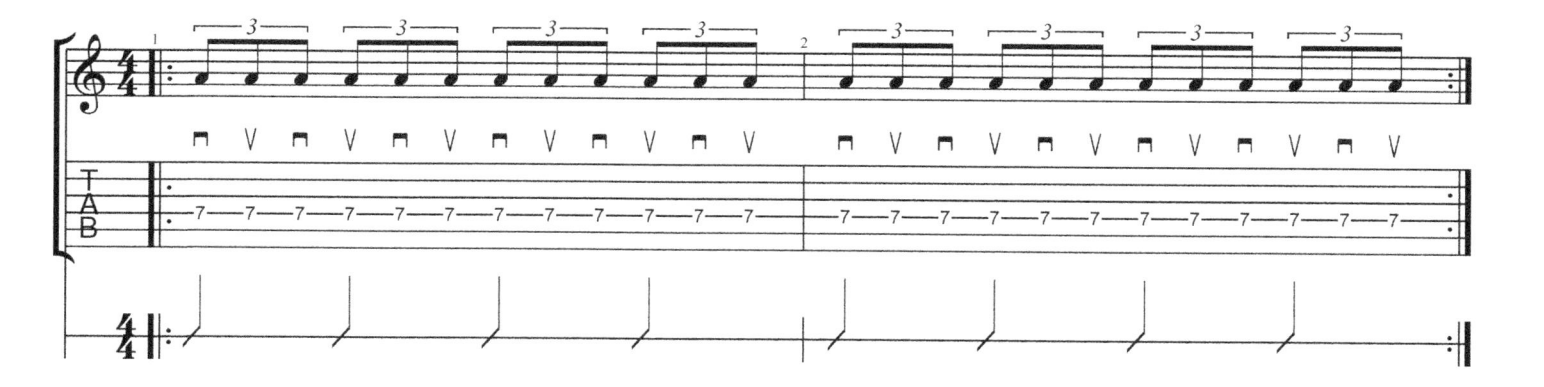

1/16th note triplets (often called *sextuplets*) are played six notes per beat (and per foot tap). They'll be twice as fast as the 1/8th note triplets from the previous example.

To emphasise the pulse, accent the downstroke on each beat using a bit more of the pick.

Example 1h:

As you combine various subdivisions within a bar, it's crucial not to lose where each beat lands. Stay locked in with your tapping foot in the following two examples as you slice up the bar with a mix of note groupings.

To emphasise the beats and reinforce the synchronization of your picking hand and tapping foot, place strong accents on notes that coincide with the clicks of the metronome.

Example 1i:

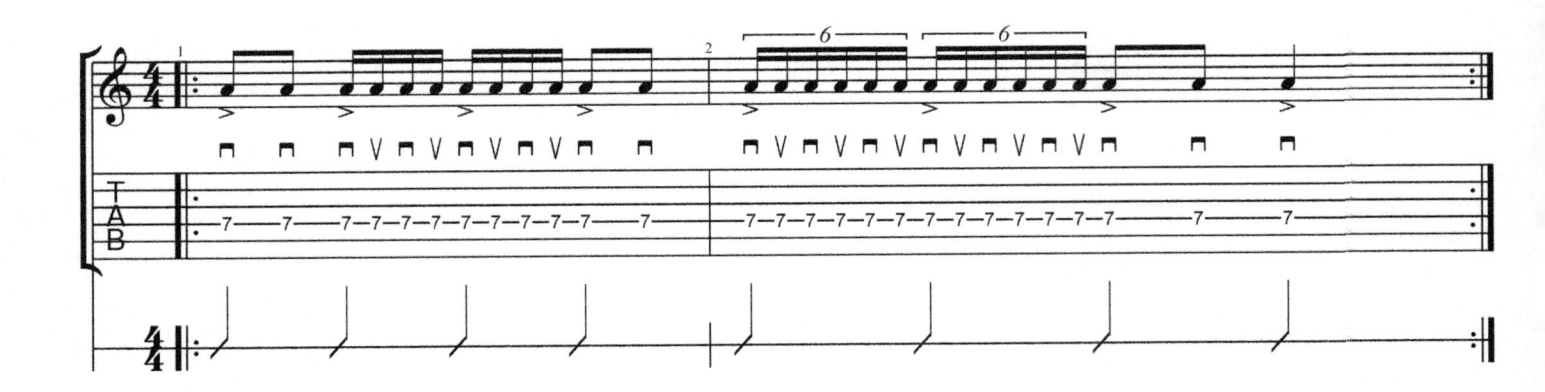

Example 1j:

Before moving to the next chapter, it's important to spend some time baking the critical areas of this chapter into your playing.

- Tapping the foot opposite to your picking hand
- Foot-tapping 1/4 notes along with the metronome
- Comparing toe-taps, heel-toe taps, and toe-heel taps.
- Dividing the beat in several ways with the picking hand while maintaining a solid foot-tap.

Do these exercises justice as they'll give you a firm foundation for what follows. When you're ready, let's begin the next step of synchronization by combining picking with single-string fretting hand motifs.

Chapter Two: Single String Synchronization

In this chapter, we'll work on synchronizing the picking and fretting hands using chromatic drills you can (and should) practice on every string.

You'll no longer see the rhythmic notation of the metronome and foot taps in the tabs, as it's assumed you now have that discipline happening.

Before you grab that guitar pick, however, let's make sure we can lock the fretting hand into our tapping foot, synchronizing two limbs on the same side of the body this time.

For Example 2a, create light hammer-ons from nowhere (indicated as fretting hand taps with a circled T) to hear if you're fretting each note in time. Fingers one to four will press down the G string, one digit at a time, without pick strokes.

There's no need to stack all the fingers down cumulatively, since most real-world playing doesn't involve putting four fingers on the fretboard to play one note.

To begin, anchor your thumb behind the neck for good leverage, then hammer the index finger on the 5th fret of the G string, holding it for two beats.

Hammer the second finger on the 6th fret, lifting the index finger off when you've made contact, like passing the baton in a relay race. Continue with the other fingers in the same fashion. To offset the different finger lengths, watch the video to see how I *roll* the fingers of my fretting hand onto the board.

The goal is to place each finger down precisely on the relevant tap of your foot, not before or after.

Example 2a:

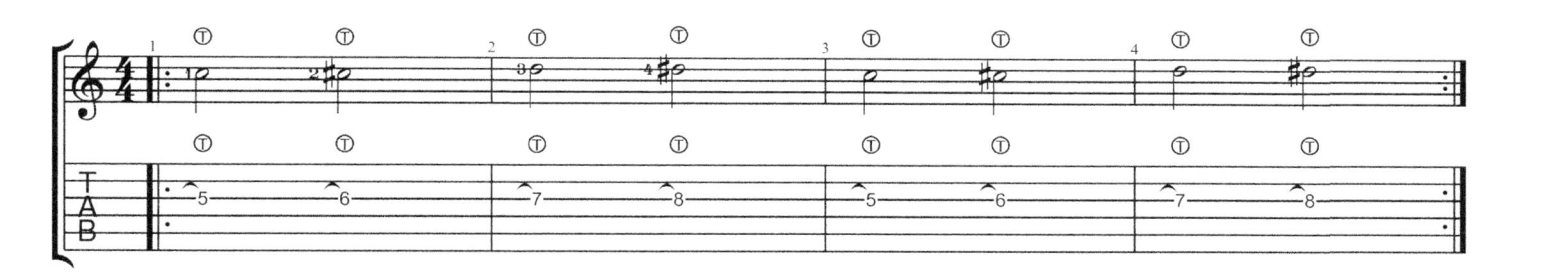

Next, press the notes down in 1/4 note (Example 2b) and 1/8th note (Example 2c) intervals. Expand the following two drills by moving them to each string, maintaining foot taps all the way through.

Example 2b:

Example 2c:

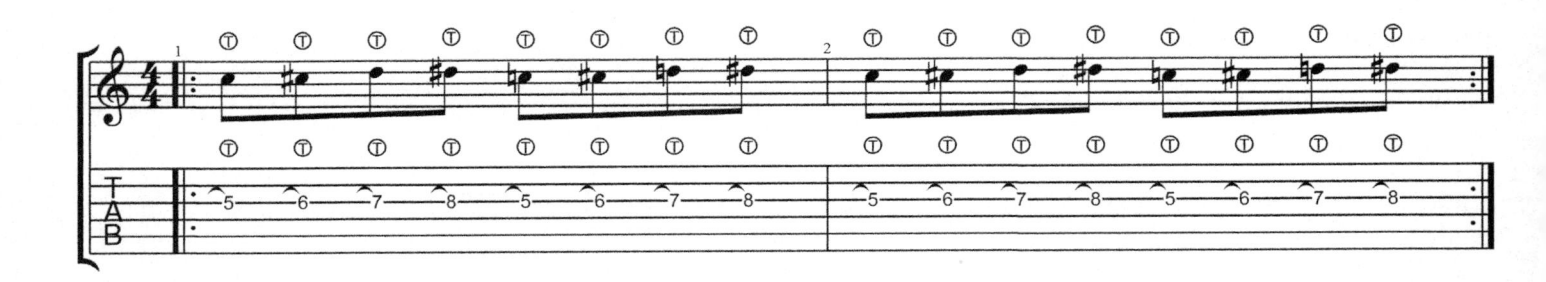

If you placed each finger down with good timing in the last three examples, re-introduce the pick.

In the next section, we'll use picking drills to solidify the connection between picking and fretting hands.

Chromatic Synchronization Picking Drills

Using good finger placement timing, let's pick a combination of 1/16th and 1/4 notes with the same fretting – two pitches per bar.

You can begin with the index finger already in place in bar one, but the other fingers will need to land on new frets in sync with each downstroke.

You want to avoid creating a *flam* sound, where a note accidentally sounds twice in quick succession because either a pick stroke or fretted note occurs too early or too late.

Example 2d:

Let's keep the picking going this time and change notes on each beat. Focus on synchronizing each note change with the picking hand.

Bonus physicality tip: gently nod your head on each beat for another degree of body synchronization.

Example 2e:

Changing positions is an important area of synchronization. On the B string in Example 2f, the index finger starts bar one on the 3rd fret, jumps to the 7th fret in the next bar, and so on.

Making each position shift on time is essential, so begin very slow and use your eyes to focus on each new position before you move there.

The shifting transitions won't always sound seamless, but as a synchronization exercise, the aim is to shift positions without interrupting the steady repetition of the picking hand. If you're stopping and starting the picking motion, your fretting hand probably isn't keeping up.

Avoid sliding into each position. Do your best to launch into every spot with a clean placement of the index finger, sliding your thumb behind the neck too.

Example 2f:

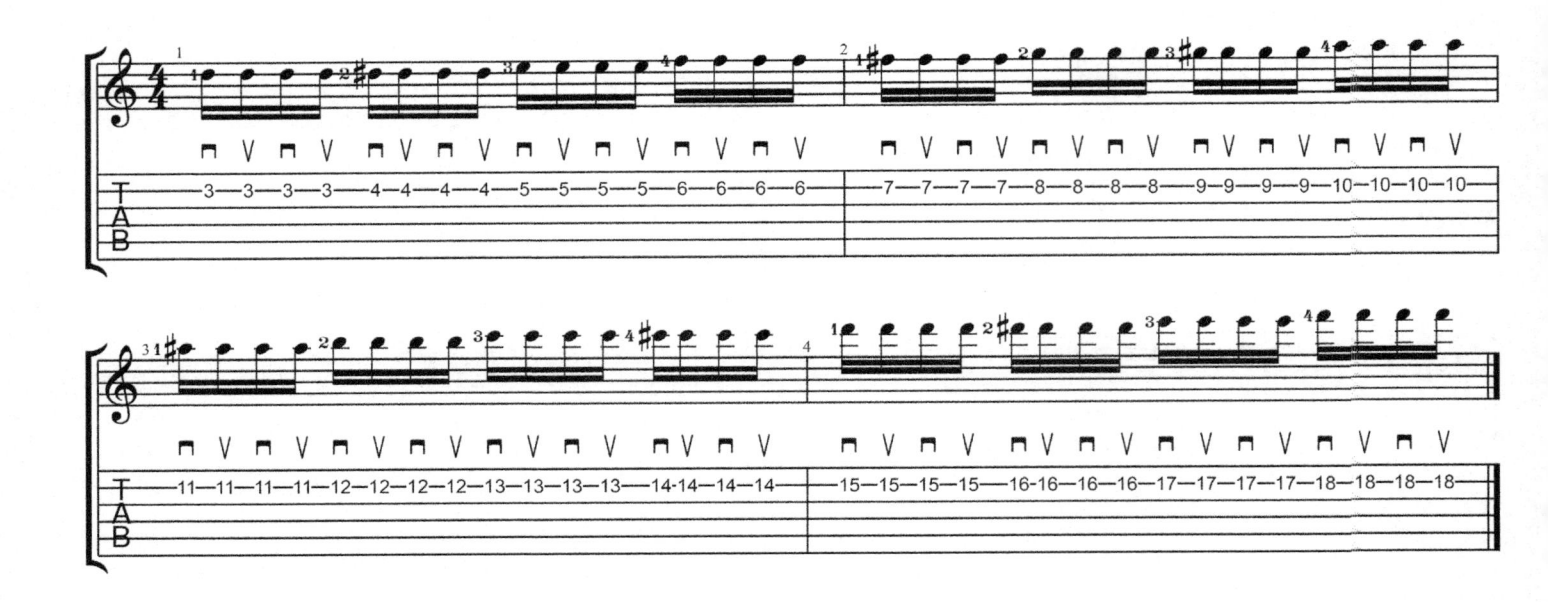

Let's work on ascending index finger and descending pinkie finger leaps in one exercise. I'm moving to the D string for this drill, but I suggest using every string for versatility.

Keep an eye out for the finger slides at the end of each bar, and be sure not to play any note more or less than twice.

Example 2g:

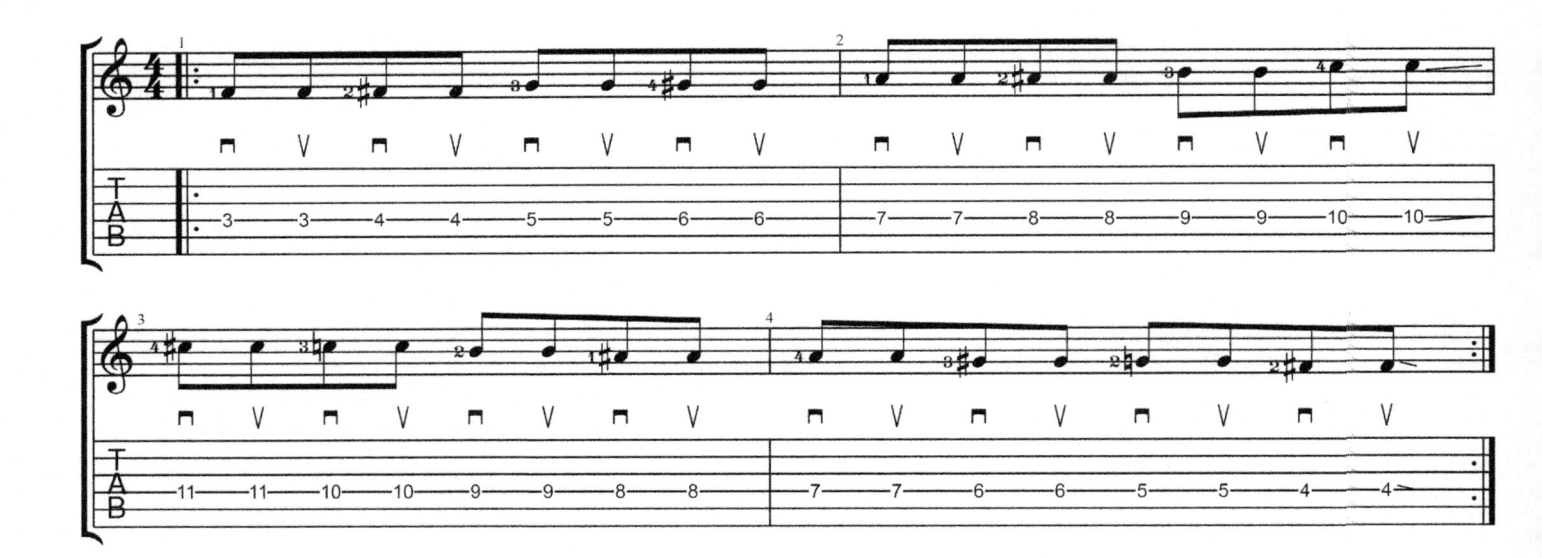

Putting unusual twists on more conventional picking drills is another excellent way to build synchronization and become more adaptable. By deviating from what your mind or hands might be expecting, you develop greater versatility to tackle whatever comes.

We'll reconfigure some previous drills to create new challenges for the next few examples. Some will feel slightly upside down until you become as comfortable with them as the straightforward versions.

Here's a tweak of Example 2e, which began each new note on a beat and with a downstroke.

Removing one C note on the 5th fret of the G string to the end of the bar means each new pitch occurs on the last 1/16th note of each beat. New notes now occur on upstrokes.

The picking hand will still be locked in with your tapping foot, but the challenge is to change notes with the fretting hand in new spots without reverting to the previous version.

Take it nice and slow to begin with, as it may feel upside down at first.

Example 2h:

The other upstroke where we can change notes is the second 1/16th note of each beat.

Example 2i:

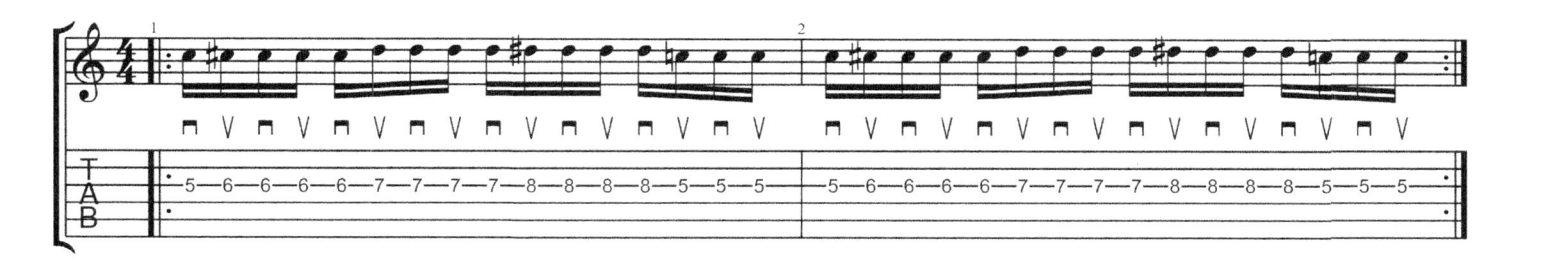

Example 2j reconfigures the notes of Example 2g but with 1/8th notes.

Bar one begins with a single F note on the D string, and the rest will feel a bit topsy turvy as the notes change on the *and* of each beat, and with opposite pick strokes to before. Factoring in the slides and position jumps, you'll have several things to consider and lock-in!

Example 2j:

Here's another spin on Example 2e with multiple changes to look out for.

Played on the A string, 1/16th notes are replaced by 1/8th note triplets, and the notes also change in threes. The fun of this drill is in the displaced feel of bars three and four, contrasting the straightforwardness of bars one and two. Watch your fretting finger timing in the second half.

Example 2k:

18

Finger Independence

A common cause of being out-of-sync is feeling like some fingers (or combinations of fingers) refuse to co-operate. That can lead to timing issues, an inconsistent sound, or compromised ability.

We can remedy such issues with exercises that focus on specific hurdles. Whatever the hurdle, there's bound to be a drill you can construct to highlight, correct, and eliminate the problem.

Take adjacent fingers, for example. Fingers two and three, or three and four, can be targeted directly in drills to improve separation.

Example 2l targets three pairs of adjacent fingers. A 1/2 note rest at the end of bars two and four allows a moment to let go of any strain that might otherwise accumulate.

Example 2l:

Which finger pair did you find the most troublesome in the previous example? That will be the focus of a new exercise.

If fingers two and three felt slower or more cumbersome than the others, we can emphasise the problem in a new drill and use that to out-practice the issue.

Example 2m:

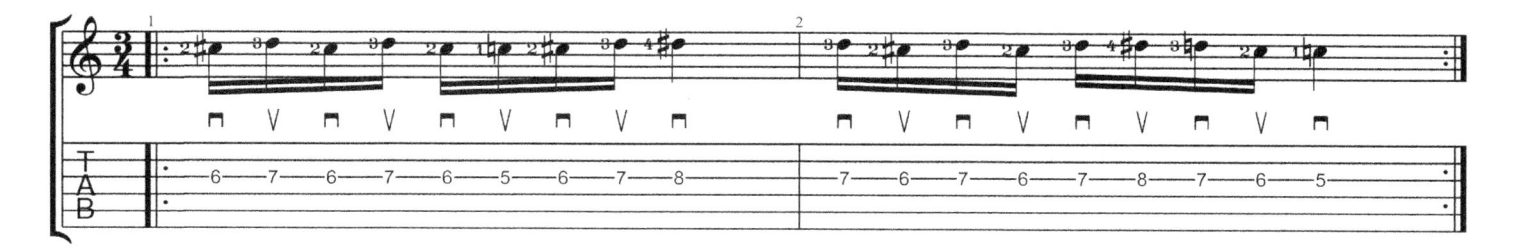

19

If it was the third and fourth finger combo, try this.

Example 2n:

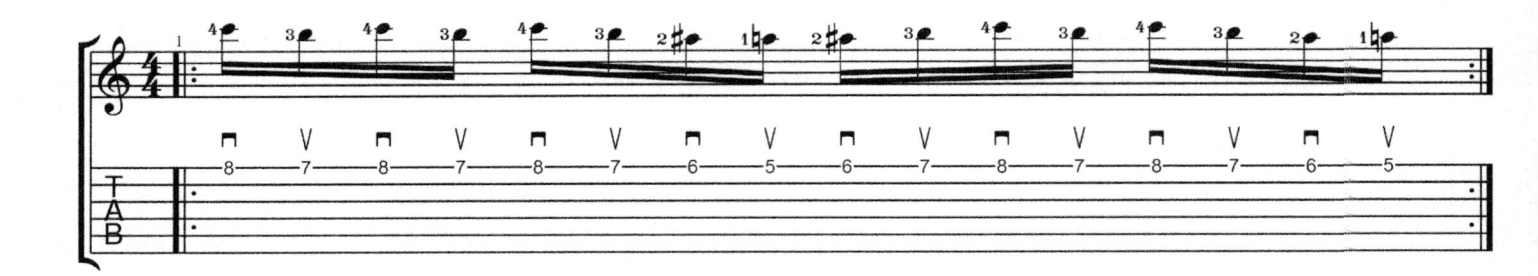

The twenty-four permutations of 1-2-3-4

With common chromatic exercises where fingers one to four are played in order on each string, you can become accustomed to pairing fingers with pick strokes. Like the 1-2-3-4 drills, for example, where downstrokes are always paired with fingers one and three and upstrokes are assigned to fingers two and four.

There are twenty-four combinations in which we can arrange the numbers one, two, three, and four, each occurring once. These are known in guitar teaching circles as *the twenty-four permutations*.

To run through the permutations, choose a position of the neck where it's comfortable to play. "1" will be wherever you place your index finger, with the three frets after that being the position of fingers two, three, and four.

If your fretting hand is tripping up on some of the less standard fingerings, practice those harder ones as hammer-on-only exercises before picking them.

1-2-3-4	1-2-4-3	1-3-2-4	1-3-4-2	1-4-2-3	1-4-3-2
2-1-3-4	2-1-4-3	2-3-1-4	2-3-4-1	2-4-1-3	2-4-3-1
3-1-2-4	3-1-4-2	3-2-1-4	3-2-4-1	3-4-1-2	3-4-2-1
4-1-2-3	4-1-3-2	4-2-1-3	4-2-3-1	4-3-1-2	4-3-2-1

We'll cover alternate picking string changing in detail in Chapter Four, but if you're ready for multi-string variations of the twenty-four permutations, you can also begin putting string changes in the middle of each group of four.

Example 2o is a 1-2-3-4 drill beginning on the 7th fret. The fourth note of each row is relocated to an adjacent string – a higher string on the way up and a lower string on the way down.

Example 2o:

That was an excellent idea, so let's do it with the other fingers.

Example 2p displaces the third finger, and examples 2q and 2r displace the second and first fingers, respectively.

If you repeated the exercise with the other permutations in this manner, you'd have ninety-six different versions to choose from in your practice, and that's just using one string change in every four notes. I never want to hear you complain that you don't have anything to practice again!

Example 2p:

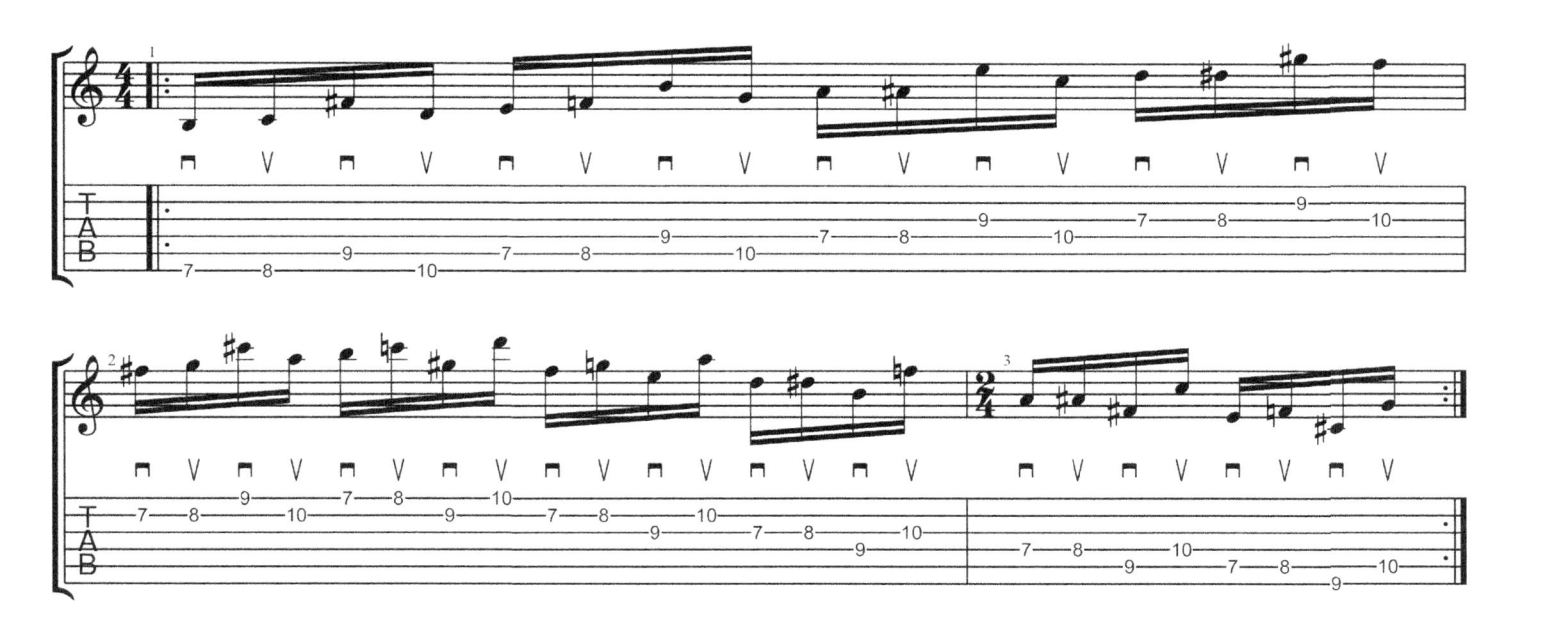

Example 2q:

Example 2r:

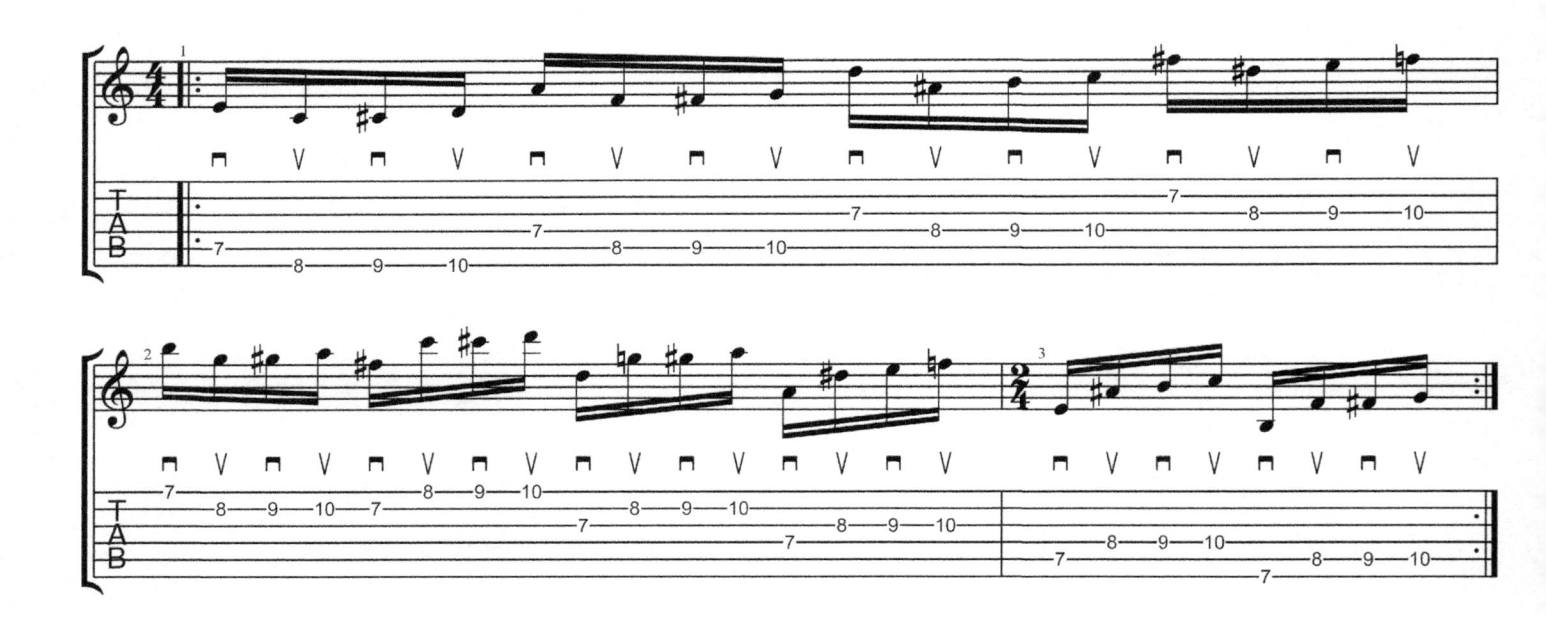

See what other twists you can come up with. The aim is to find a challenge related to synchronization or control of the fingers and use it to improve both. Discard the exercise when it becomes comfortable and choose another one to take its place.

The next chapter will utilise major and minor scales for musical synchronization applications.

Chapter Three: Diatonic Cells and Permutations

It's time to delve into diatonic major and minor scale fragments that you're much more likely to see in musical situations.

In this chapter, we'll put twists on different melodic groups to challenge and improve the synchronization of fretting hand fingers, using single-string motifs and sequences. In Chapter Four, we'll level up by exploring string changes and their effect on the synchronization we create here.

Ways to improve synchronization with scale notes include:

- Exploring common scale fragments
- Creating different "lock-in" points
- Increasing the difficulty of drills to improve focus and attention to detail
- Moving up and down strings diatonically using position shifts

All diatonic examples in the rest of the book use the C Major scale and its relative minor scale, A Minor, unless otherwise stated. Across the fretboard, the notes look like this:

Figure 1:

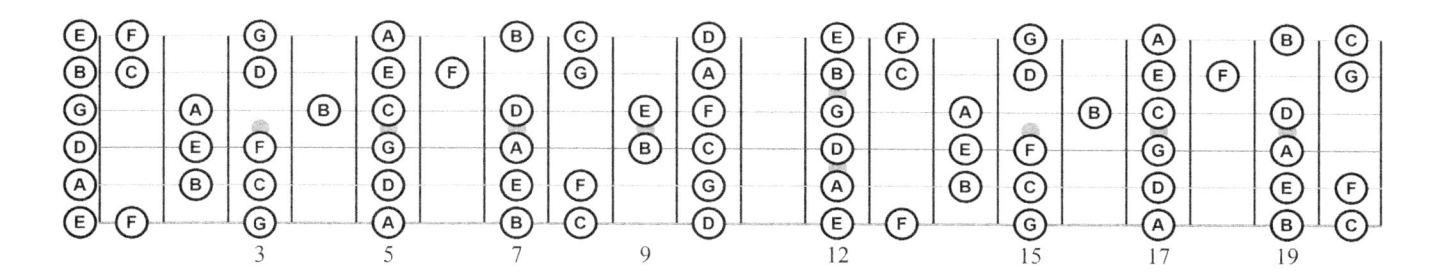

Let's begin with some three-note scale fragments, which we'll apply to motifs constructed from between three and seven notes.

As you can see in the above diagram, any group of three notes along one string is made up of either a whole tone plus a semitone (A, B, C, and D, E, F), a semitone plus a whole tone (B, C, D, and E, F, G), or two consecutive whole tones (C, D, E, as well as F, G, A, and G, A, B).

The first thing we can do with three notes is repeat them in ascending order. Example 3a repeats the notes E, F, and G on the G string. Each triplet group begins on a pick stroke opposite to the next.

Spend measured practice time on this pattern, then turn off your metronome and accelerate the phrase to the edge of your ability, keeping the picking accents on the 9th fret E notes.

Example 3a:

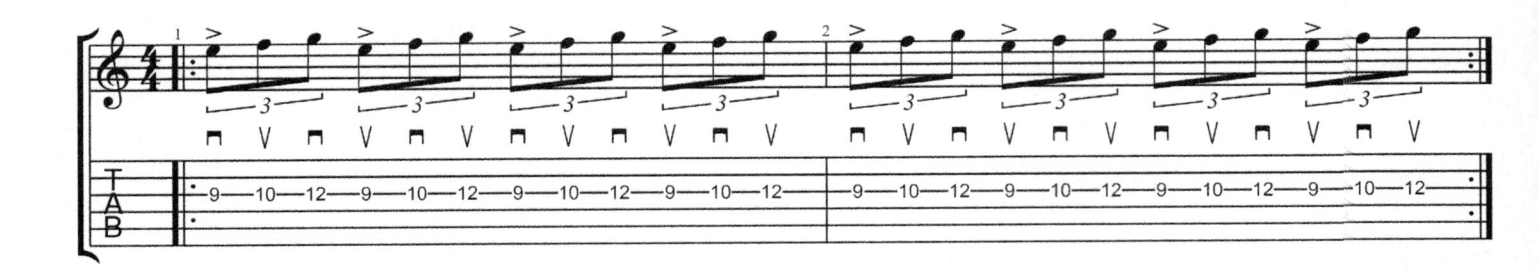

Now loop the same notes beginning from the F note on the 10th fret. Do you still feel locked in and synchronized when you speed up, or is your brain trying to reset the idea so that the E note is always on the beat?

Example 3b:

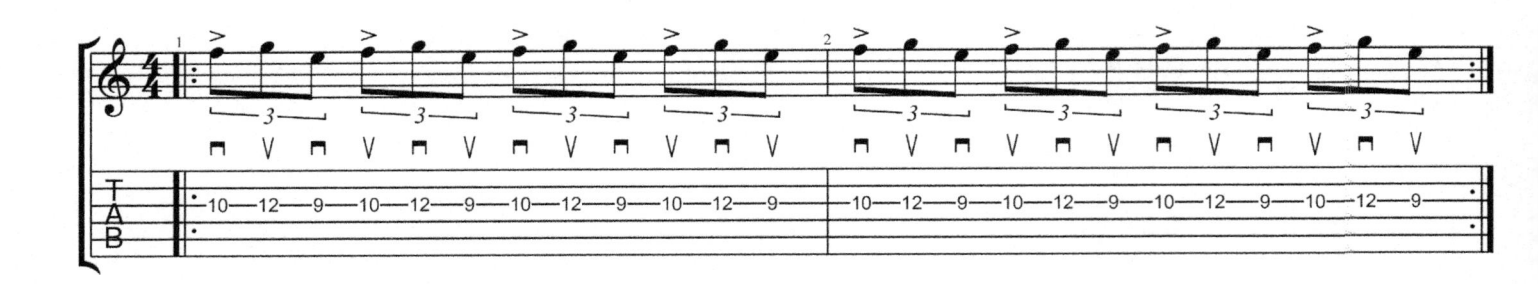

Examples 3a and 3b contain the same notes and an even distribution of downstrokes and upstrokes for each note.

But, if you felt like Example 3b was "out-of-whack", it's probably because your synchronization in Example 3a was tied to leading with the index finger.

This makes a great case for practicing permutations and experimenting with new lock-in points. When you do the work, you build adaptability into your technique.

Here's another version, starting from the G note on the 12th fret, giving us another lock-in point to practice.

Example 3c:

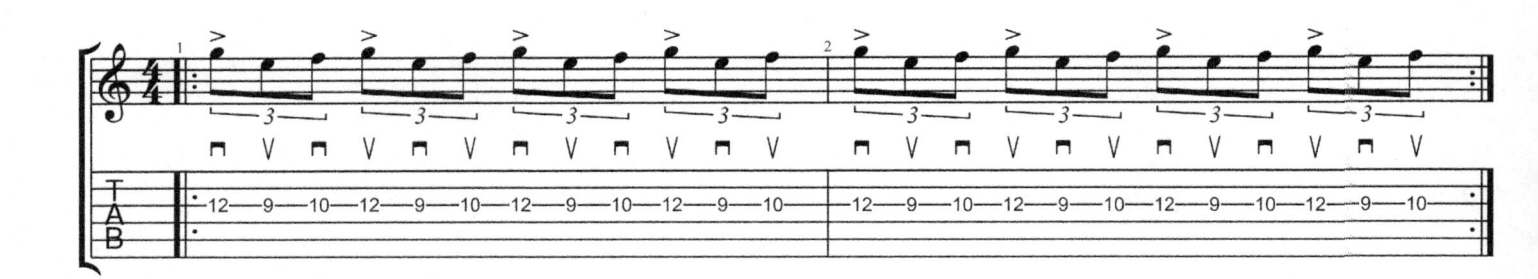

Examining permutations and lock-in points for weaknesses in synchronization can be done with descending loops too.

Here are three descending versions in one drill. Determine which permutations are weakest and invest more practice time in them.

Example 3d:

With the notes D, E, and F on the 7th, 9th, and 10th frets, Example 3e contains permutations of a four-note motif. Each bar has a different starting note and lock-in point for accenting.

Ensure that each one is synchronized, paying close attention to any attempt by your brain to reset the idea or change the pick strokes.

Example 3e:

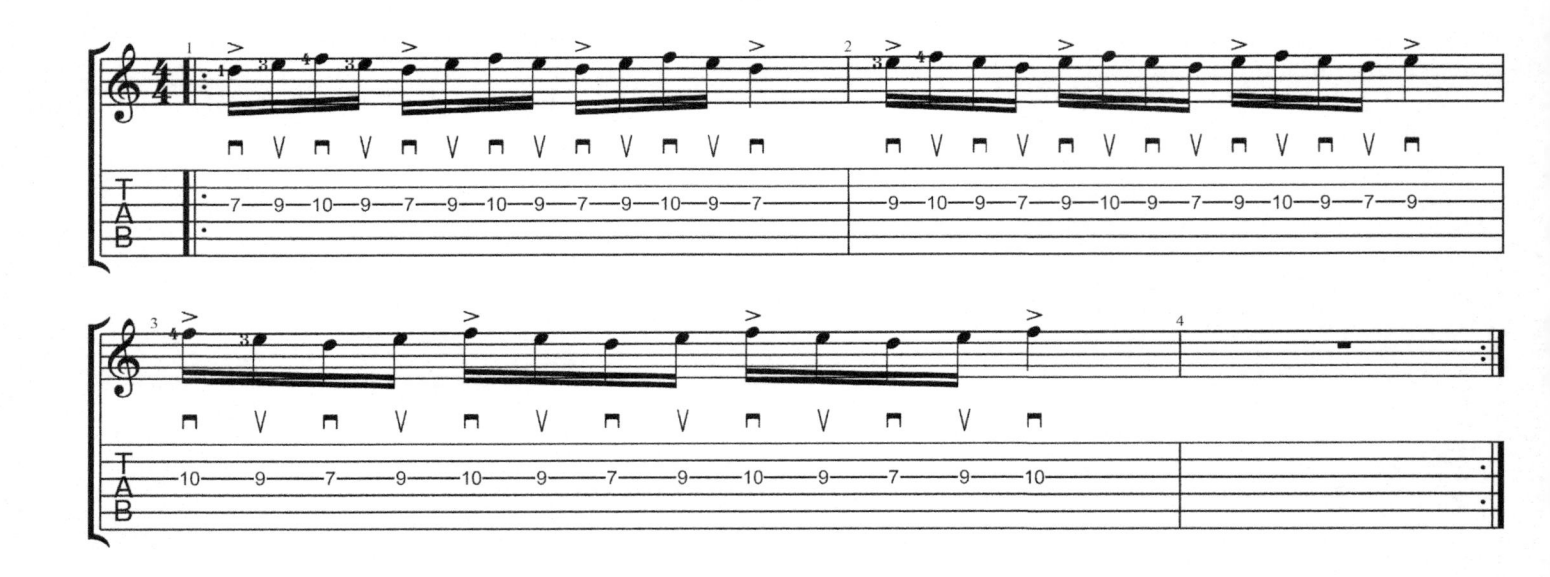

Pivoting licks are often a good synchronization test, especially if we put a little twist on one.

Example 3f begins with a motif that pedals a C note on the 10th fret of the D string between each of the A notes (7th fret) and B notes (9th fret). This alone is good synchronization practice.

A twist in bar two occurs as the phrase now begins on the pedalled C note. It's like removing the A note from bar one and reversing the pick strokes for the remaining notes.

Bars three and four are transposed downward by one diatonic step. You can turn this into an extended exercise by beginning on any string and working your way down or up through every melodic position along the string.

Example 3f:

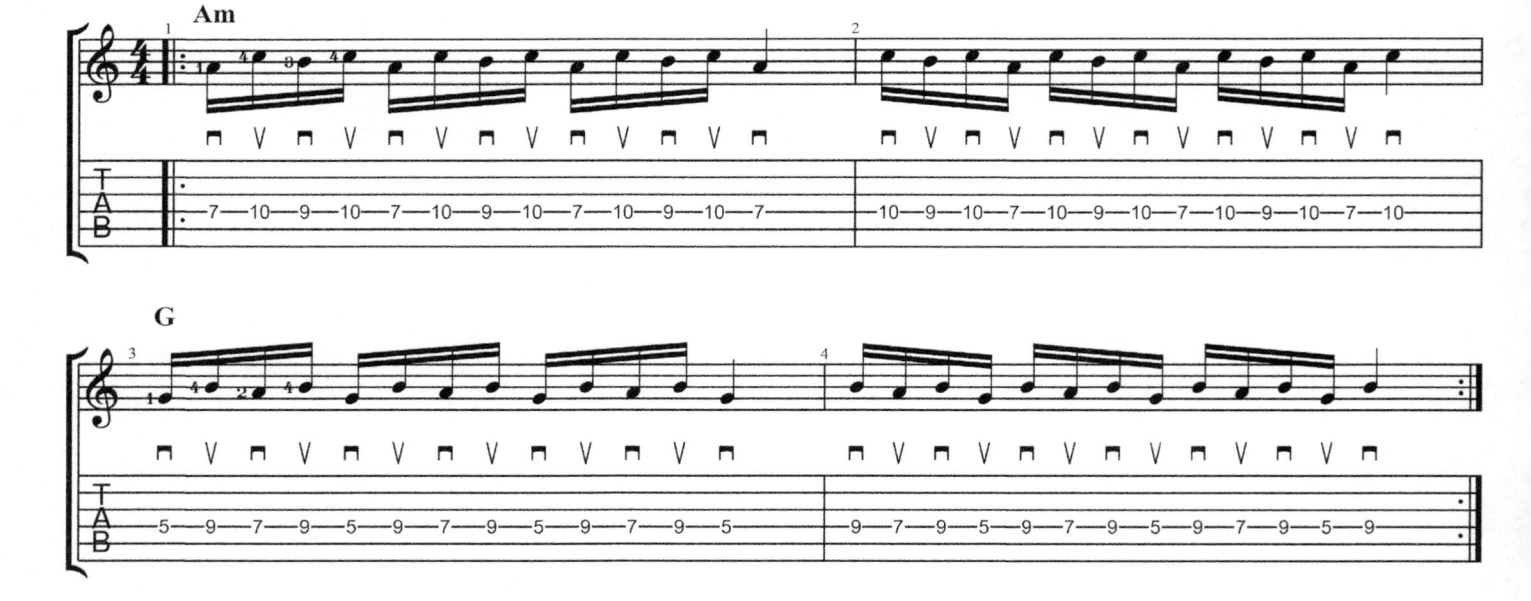

In six-note figures, a couple that really helped in my formative years can be seen in examples 3g and 3h.

The first moves up the B string, staying in the key of C Major throughout. Differing from drills like Example 3a, the six-note pattern isn't the same three notes played twice in the same direction.

Example 3g:

```
Em
|5-8-6-5-6-8-5-8-6-5-6-8-5-8-6-5-6-8-5|

F
|6-10-8-6-8-10-6-10-8-6-8-10-6-10-8-6-8-10-6|

G
|8-12-10-8-10-12-8-12-10-8-10-12-8-12-10-8-10-12-8|

Am
|10-13-12-10-12-13-10-13-12-10-12-13-10-13-12-10-12-13-10|
```

Here's the reverse counterpart of the previous drill. In this version, the pinkie finger leads each group of six notes. The line moves down the B string through the same melodic groups.

Example 3h:

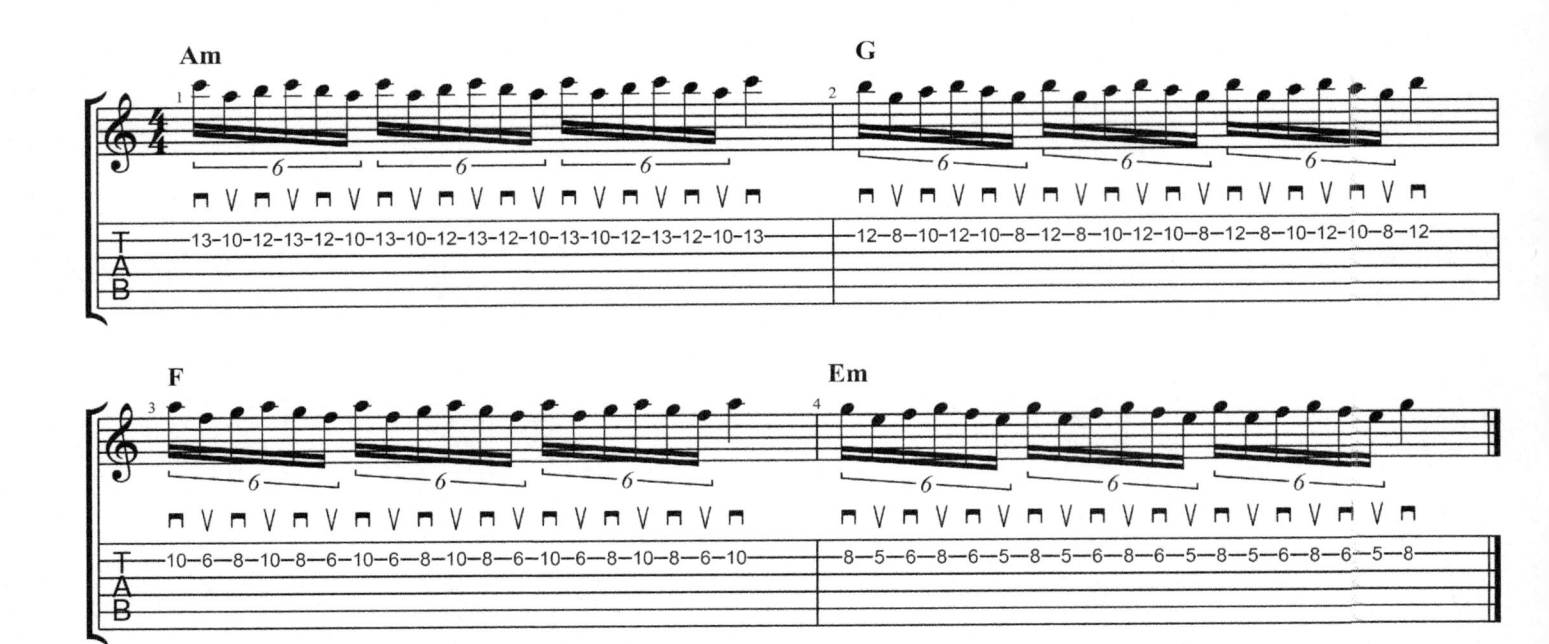

[Musical notation and tablature showing four bars with chords Am, G, F, Em. Each bar contains three groups of sextuplet sixteenth notes with alternate picking indicators (⊓ V ⊓ V ⊓ V ⊓ V ⊓ V ⊓ V ⊓ V ⊓ V ⊓ V).

Bar 1 (Am): 13-10-12-13-10-12-13-10-12-13-12-10-13-10-12-13-12-10-13
Bar 2 (G): 12-8-10-12-10-8-12-8-10-12-10-8-12-8-10-12-10-8-12
Bar 3 (F): 10-6-8-10-8-6-10-6-8-10-8-6-10-6-8-10-8-6-10
Bar 4 (Em): 8-5-6-8-6-5-8-5-6-8-6-5-8-5-6-8-6-5-8]

We've seen how changing the order of the notes, or the pick strokes linked with them, can provide a helpful area of focus for synchronization. Being able to synchronize *anything* is reliant upon versatility.

Repeated odd number motifs are a good opportunity to see the real-time challenge and reward of flipping pick strokes. Look at this five-note lick, initiated the first time with a downstroke and the second time with an upstroke.

Example 3i:

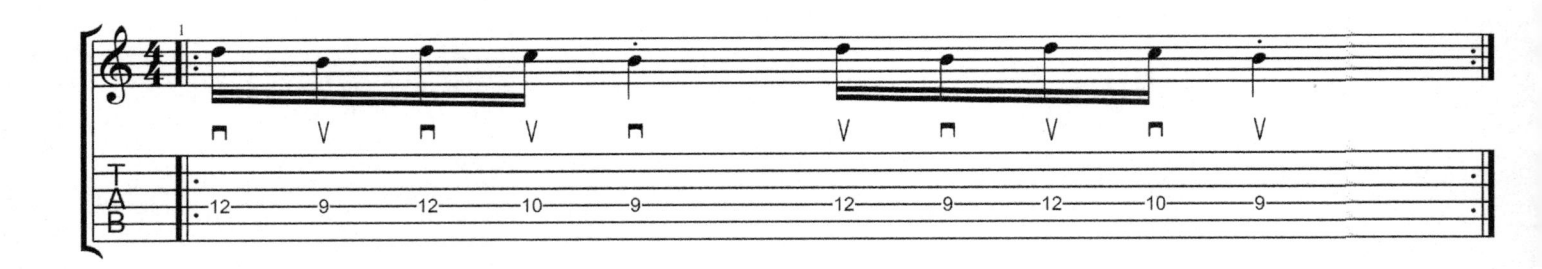

[Musical notation and tablature showing a bar with notes picked: ⊓ V ⊓ V ⊓ V ⊓ V ⊓ V
Tab: 12-9-12-10-9-12-9-12-10-9]

Let's combine a steadier stream of 1/16th notes using the same five notes. We can fit three of the five-note groups into one bar. As you'll feel, the middle group begins on an upstroke and the group on either side with a downstroke.

Example 3j:

Let's up the stakes with another five-note group, this time played across the bar line until the rest in bar two. Repeat it for as many times as you can hold it together.

Accent markers indicate where each group begins as you repeat the fives with opposite pick strokes to the group before.

Tap your foot throughout, keeping the picking hand locked into the foot taps and remembering that the pairing of fingers and pick strokes flip every five notes.

If you can execute this phrase at a moderate tempo and stay synchronized, it's a great sign that you're developing the multitasking required to coordinate unconventional phrases without getting thrown off.

Example 3k:

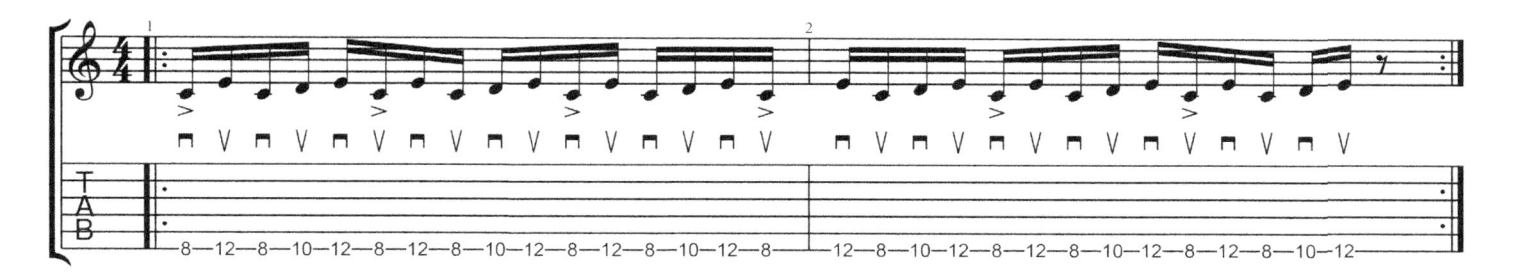

Before we move on to position-shifting, concluding this section is a seven-note repeated motif, played as 1/16th notes. Try moving this around to any position or string.

Avoid the temptation to tap your foot at the beginning of each seven, remembering that the rhythms are still 1/16th notes, and the beat is still based on 1/4 notes.

Example 3l:

Synchronized Position Shifts

For diatonic scales, position changes use a mix of intervals that need to be executed in time using good hand-eye coordination.

As you work through the position-shifting drills ahead, keep two guidelines in mind:

1. Don't let the fretting hand disturb the rhythm of the picking hand
2. Execute fretting hand shifts as smoothly as possible for melodic continuity

Moving up the A Minor scale, two notes per position, Example 3m leads with the index finger, followed by either the second or third finger according to the interval.

From the 2nd position to the 5th position, the index finger shifts up by three semitones. From the 5th fret to the 9th fret, it's a four-semitone move. Regardless of the interval, the shift needs to happen in time with the picking hand and the tap of your foot or click of the metronome.

Example 3m:

For rhythmic diversity, let's rephrase the previous example as 1/8th note triplets, staying with two fingers per position.

Example 3n:

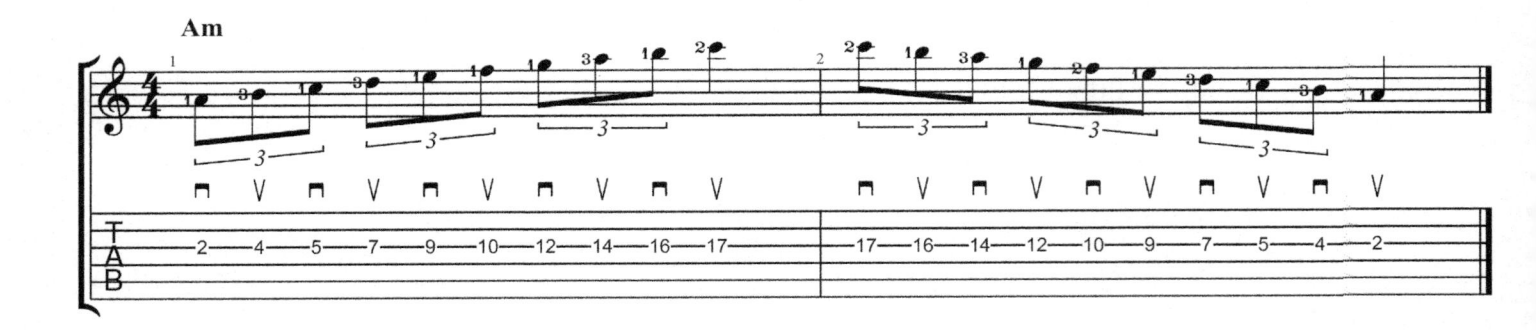

With three fingers per position, Example 3o includes larger position jumps. The index finger will shift upwards five frets each time. In the descent, the pinkie finger will shift down six frets, then five frets.

Go as slowly as necessary to ensure accurate fretting before going faster.

Example 3o:

Exploring other strings, Example 3p is an extended position-shifting drill going up and down the A string and D string, three fingers per position as indicated.

I learned to practice this on each string when taking classical guitar lessons many years ago. I've never regretted knowing my scales horizontally for connecting to vertical patterns at will, so give it a go!

Study the scale map at the beginning of the chapter to apply this drill to any string.

Example 3p:

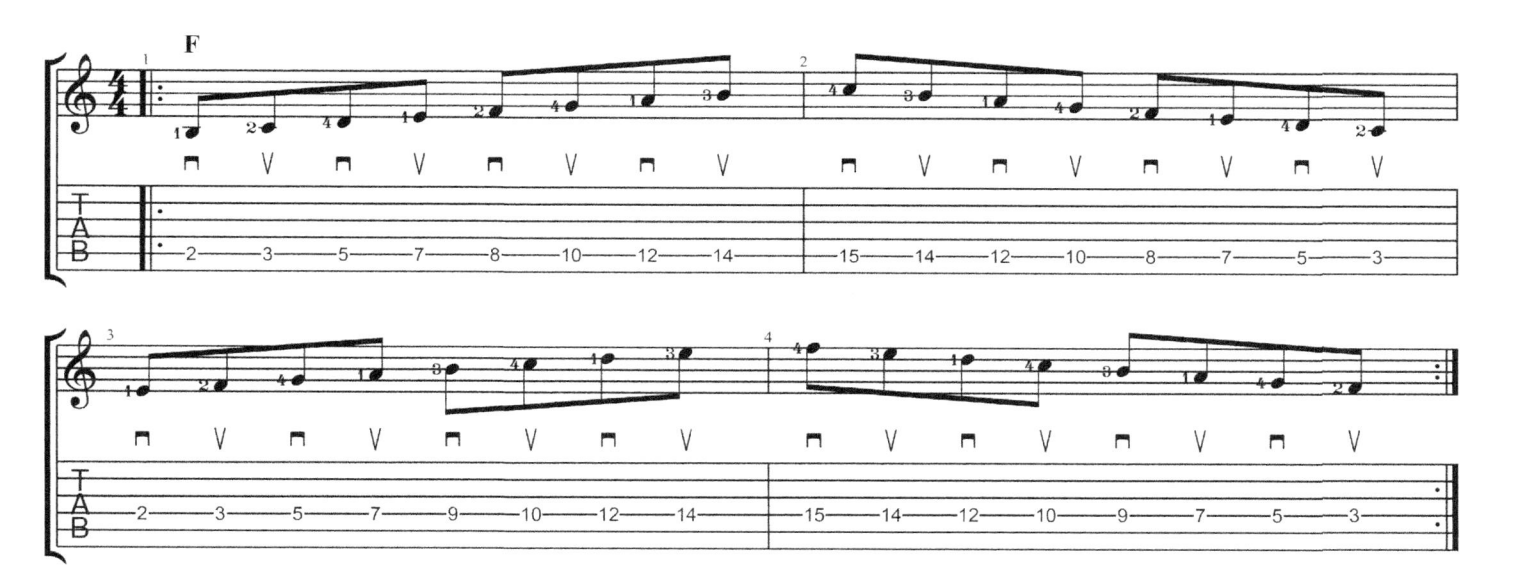

To overlap notes and create sequences along a string, try moving up and down just one note in the scale each time. Example 3q sees the index and pinkie fingers moving in whole tone and semitone leaps according to the A Minor scale notes.

Example 3q:

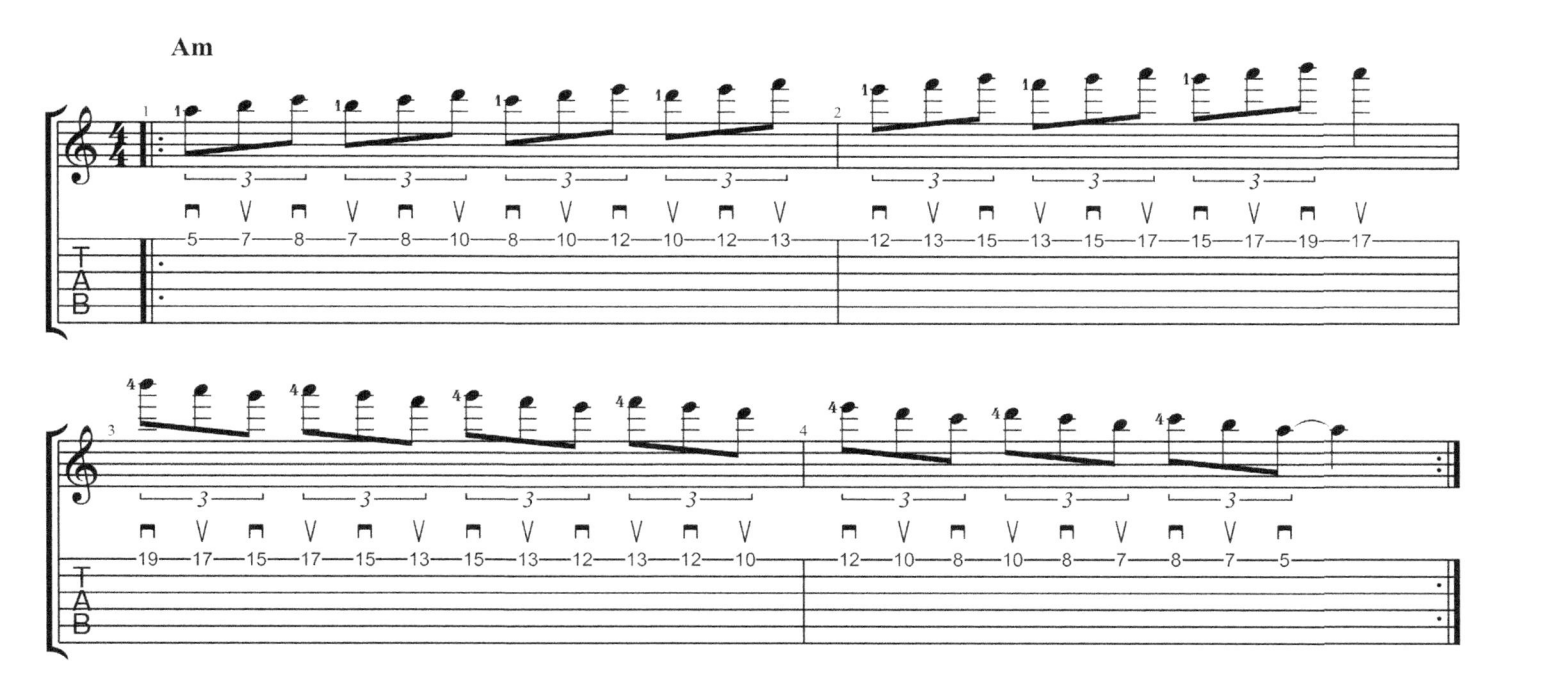

Sliding position shifts challenge timing and synchronization since the same finger is used twice on different frets.

Here's an example using pinkie slides in the ascent and index slides in the descent. Avoid sliding too early or late, and ensure that sliding notes are synchronized perfectly with the pick.

Example 3r:

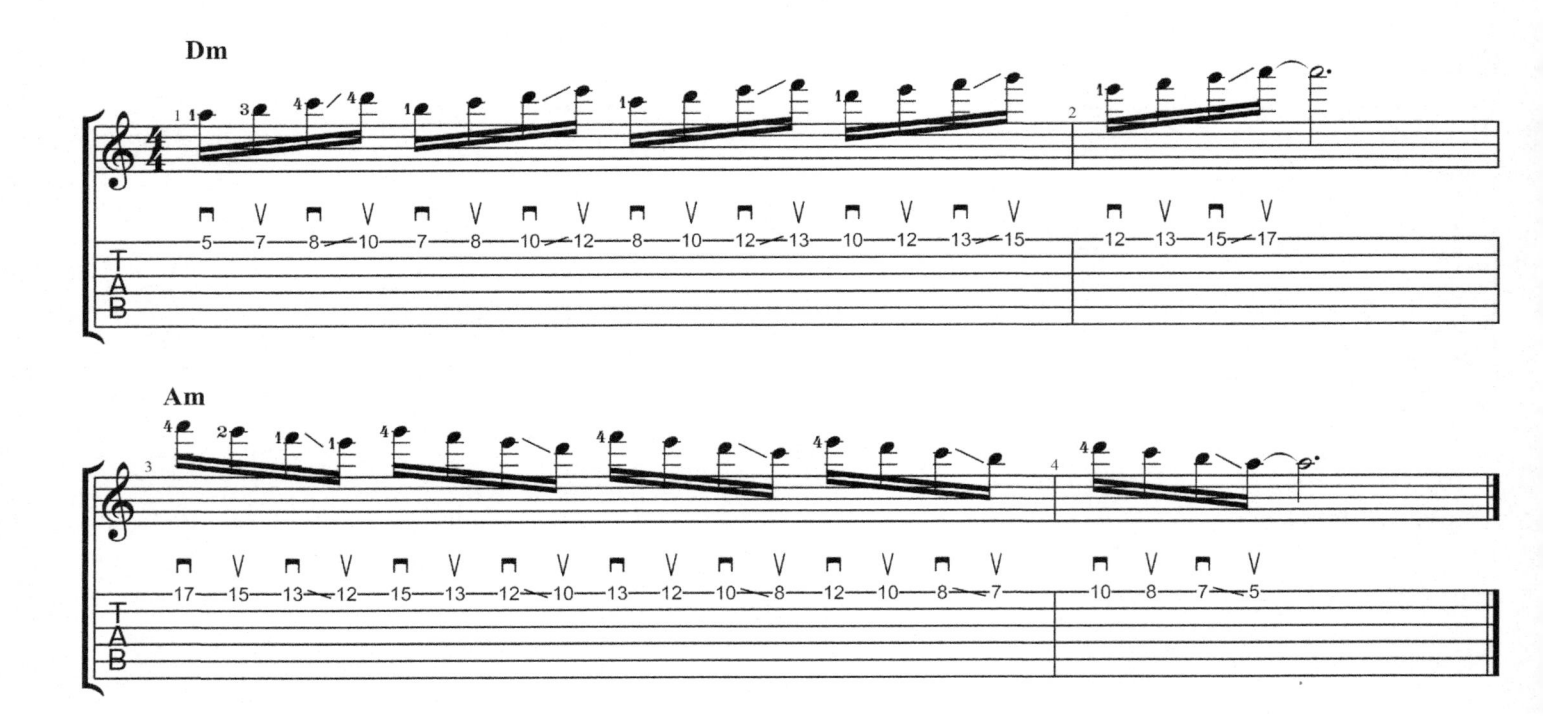

```
Dm
e|----5--7--8/10--7--8--10/12--8--10--12/13--10--12--13/15----12--13--15/17----|
   ⊓  V  ⊓  V   ⊓  V   ⊓  V  ⊓  V   ⊓  V   ⊓  V   ⊓  V    ⊓  V   ⊓  V

Am
e|--17--15--13\12--15--13--12\10--13--12--10\8--12--10--8\7----10--8--7\5----|
   ⊓  V   ⊓  V   ⊓  V   ⊓  V   ⊓  V   ⊓  V   ⊓  V   ⊓  V    ⊓  V  ⊓  V
```

The size of the slides can be increased for a greater challenge.

In bars one and two of this lick, the index finger performs descending slides in diatonic thirds and ascending slides of tones and semitones. A modified melodic motif sees the pinkie finger handling the slides in bars three and four.

Example 3s:

As a repeating slide drill, we can take advantage of the three whole tones (tritone) between the F and B notes of the C Major scale.

Example 3t:

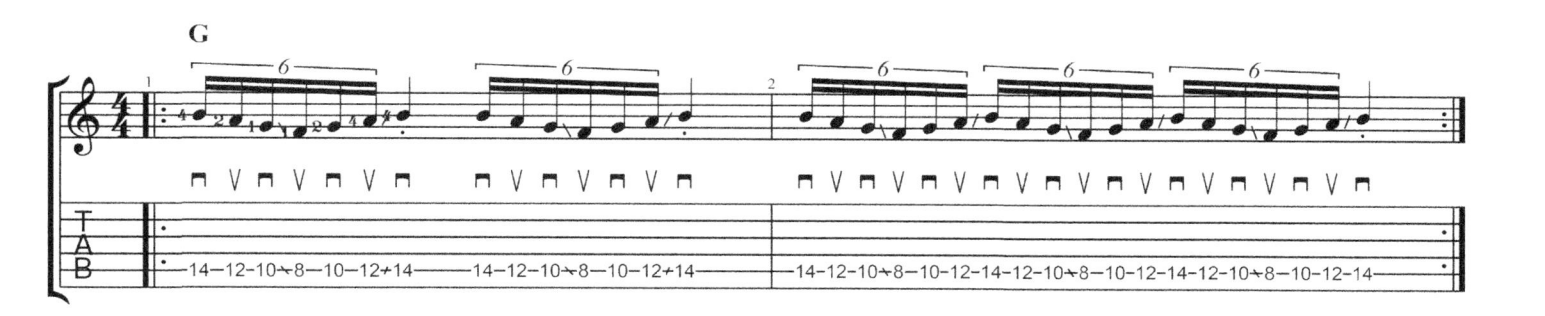

Let's take stock of your goals for this chapter

- Twisting practice drills using permutations to reveal sticking points in synchronization
- Picking three-, four-, five-, six-, and seven-note repetition drills
- Reversing pick strokes to increase versatility
- Playing unusual note groups to test your command of the beat
- Moving two- and three-note groups in position shifts along a string

- Increasing the size of position shifts
- Playing sliding position shifts in time without affecting picking hand rhythm

For areas that challenge you, construct a short daily practice routine. Even ten minutes of focused practice can untie the knots in your playing.

Choose three or four exercises per practice session, aiming to memorise the drills and perform clean and accurate repetitions. Then switch exercises when you reach the allotted time for each.

As an exercise becomes easy, it becomes less valuable, so replace redundant drills. The idea is to find something that feels uneasy, become comfortable with it, then move ahead.

In the next few chapters, we'll cover string crossing with a few different techniques, looking at ways to maximise synchronization in each.

Chapter Four will focus on alternate picking synchronization. Chapter Five delves into the unique requirements of sweep and economy picking, while Chapter Six covers legato and picking synchronization.

If you're new to these techniques, I recommend checking out the books below to immerse yourself in each technique. Rather than duplicate those texts in this space, I'll focus on each technique's synchronization requirements.

My complete technique courses are published by Fundamental Changes and include the titles:

- *Alternate Picking Guitar Technique*
- *Economy Picking Guitar Technique*
- *Sweep Picking Speed Strategies for Guitar*
- *Legato Guitar Technique Mastery*

Chapter Four: String Crossing – Alternate Picking

Let's begin with a look at the string-changing synchronization requirements of alternate picking.

For unknotting any trouble spots, I recommend an approach that I call *LIE*: *locate, isolate, exaggerate*.

- *Locate* – find the point within a lick that may be causing trouble or hindering progress
- *Isolate* – separate the issue from the rest of the lick for focused resolution
- *Exaggerate* – increase the difficulty or frequency of the issue to overcome it

This three-step process has helped me conquer many technique issues, so I'll provide examples of the approach using the material in this chapter.

You can alternate pick various ways using the wrist, elbow, forearm, and fingers. I'm going to assume that you already know how you like to pick, but the bonus video includes a little primer on these options.

Since alternate picking uses opposing pick strokes across strings, you'll encounter four combinations of string changes: two *inside picking* and two *outside picking* changes.

1. Inside: an upstroke on a lower string followed by a downstroke on a higher string
2. Inside: a downstroke on a higher string followed by an upstroke on a lower string
3. Outside: a downstroke on a lower string followed by an upstroke on a higher string
4. Outside: an upstroke on a higher string followed by a downstroke on a lower string.

Here are some small examples of the above.

Example 4a:

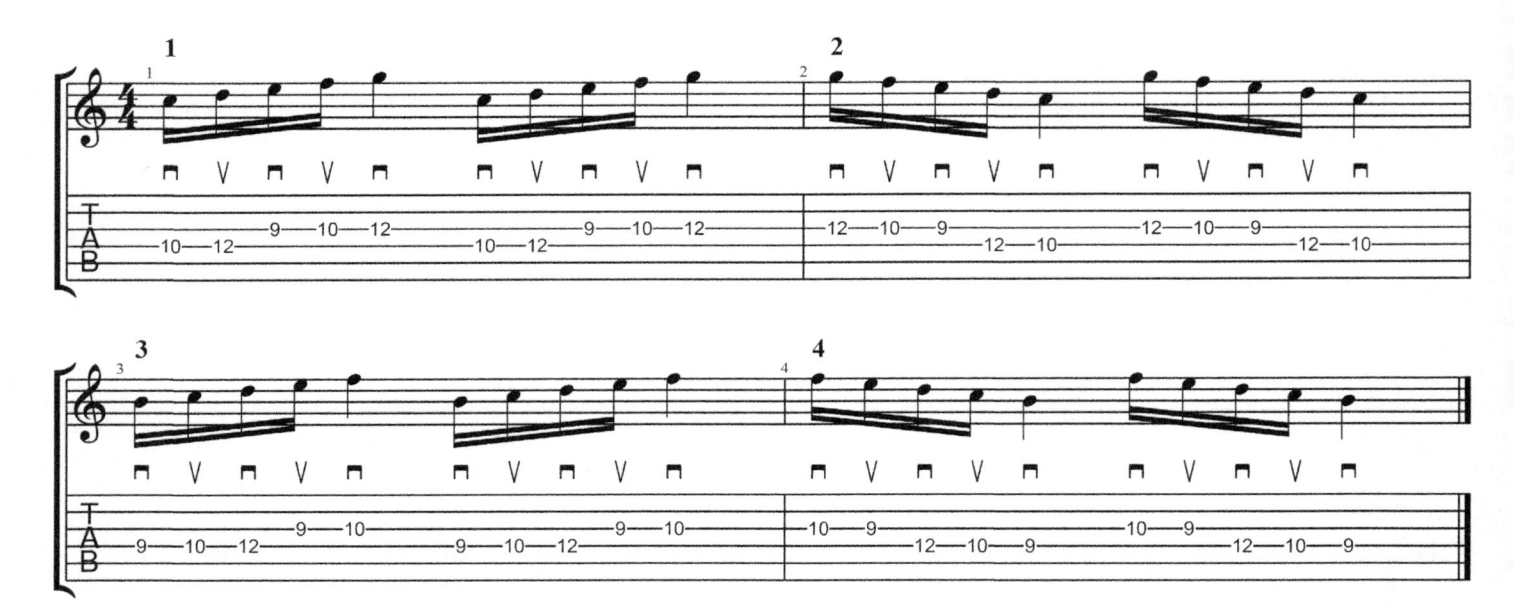

```
Bar 1:
E|-------------------------------|
B|-------------------------------|
G|-------------------------------|
D|------9--10--12-----9--10--12--|
A|--10--12--------10--12---------|
E|-------------------------------|
   ⊓ V ⊓ V ⊓  ⊓ V ⊓ V ⊓

Bar 2:
E|-------------------------------|
B|-------------------------------|
G|-------------------------------|
D|--12--10--9-----12--10--9------|
A|------12--10--------12--10-----|
E|-------------------------------|
   ⊓ V ⊓ V ⊓  ⊓ V ⊓ V ⊓

Bar 3:
D|---------9--10-------9--10-----|
A|--9--10--12------9--10--12-----|
   ⊓ V ⊓ V ⊓  ⊓ V ⊓ V ⊓

Bar 4:
D|--10--9---------10--9----------|
A|------12--10--9-----12--10--9--|
   ⊓ V ⊓ V ⊓  ⊓ V ⊓ V ⊓
```

To change strings without interrupting the synchronization and control you've achieved with single-string picking, consider the following:

- The pick needs to travel to notes on new strings with the same good timing as along one string
- The pick needs clear access to each new string
- Direct and accurate motions will keep the hands working together

Let's work through the four alternate picking string changes from the list.

Example 4b includes an inside stroke to change strings from an upstroke on the D string to a downstroke on the G string.

To accurately perform the string change in bar two, the last upstroke on the D string needs to clear the plane of the strings to go straight to the G string in time with the fretting hand's index finger. Watch me perform this lick on the bonus video for a close-up view.

As you speed up, use the single-string repetition pattern in bar one as a benchmark for what you can achieve, then play through both bars to see if the timing and synchronization hold up during the string change.

Example 4b:

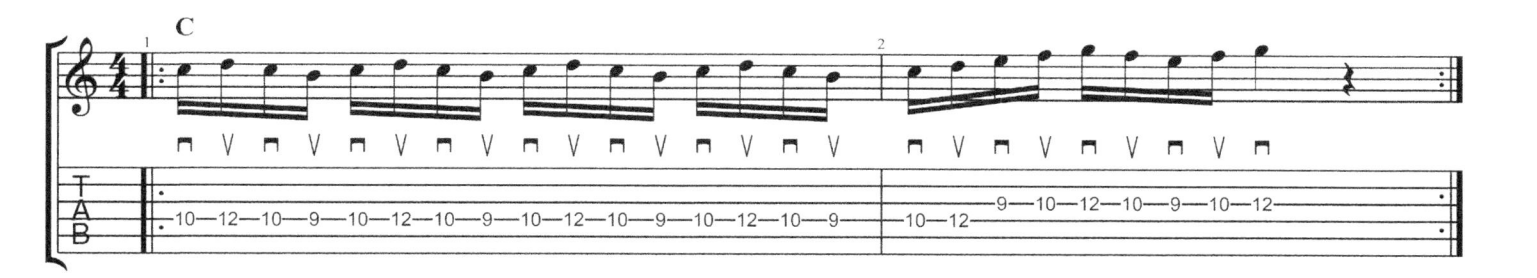

Example 4c shows how I apply the LIE approach to patterns like the previous exercise.

If the string change is the sticking point, we've already done the *locate* part. Next, we *isolate*.

To focus on hitting the first note of the G string, bars one and two isolate the string-changing element. Try picking louder than you usually do, putting an extra accent on the E note on the G string (9th fret).

In bars three and four, there's a running start before the string change. In bars five and six, more of the complete lick from Example 4b has been added. Keep accenting the string change for now.

Example 4c:

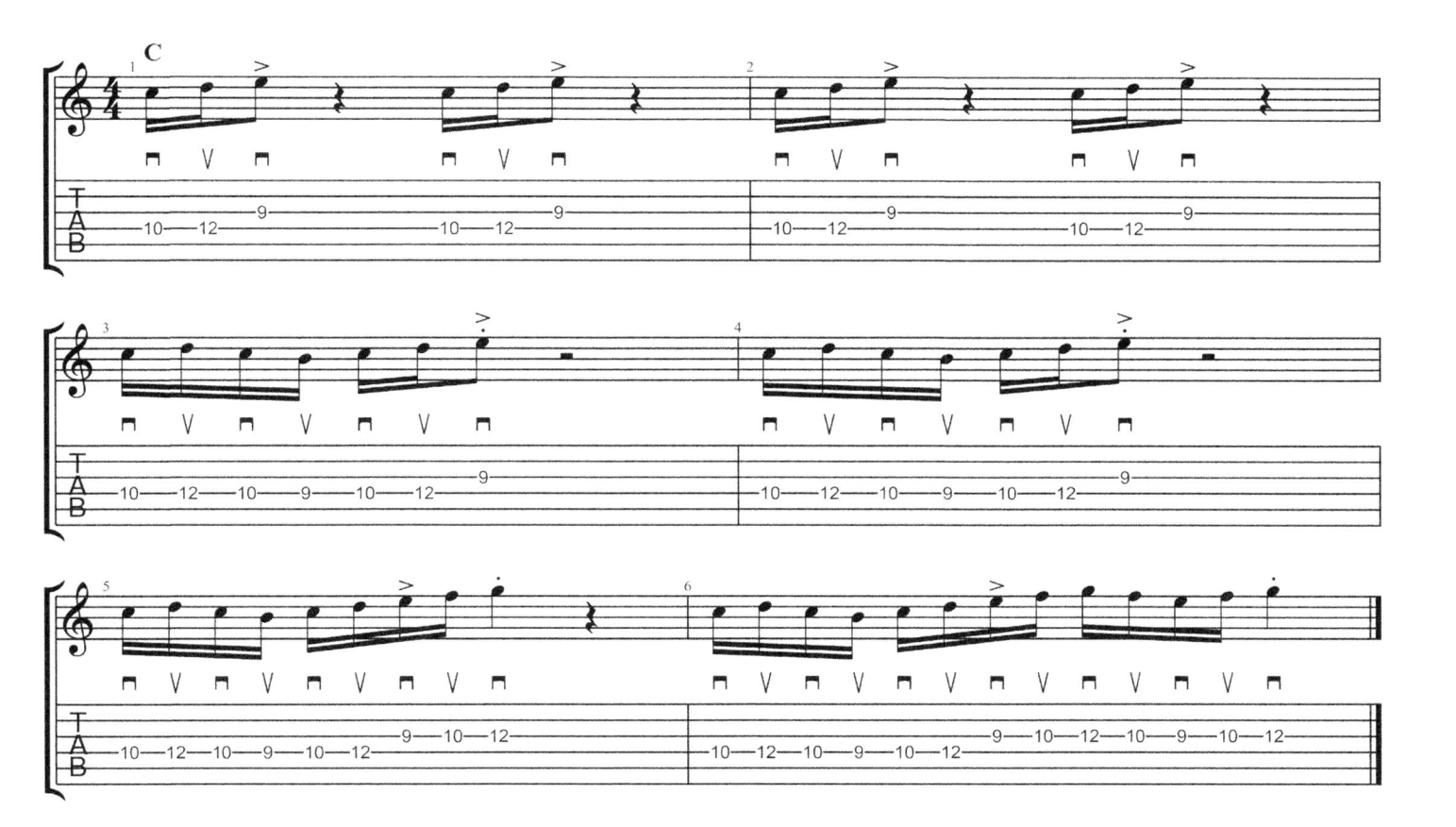

39

We can increase the distance between adjacent strings with string skipping for the exaggerated stage. The higher degree of difficulty from the D string to the B string will make adjacent string-changing easier by comparison.

If you're feeling especially adventurous, include a string skip to the high E string, shown in bars three and four. Both string skipping options stay within the key.

Example 4d:

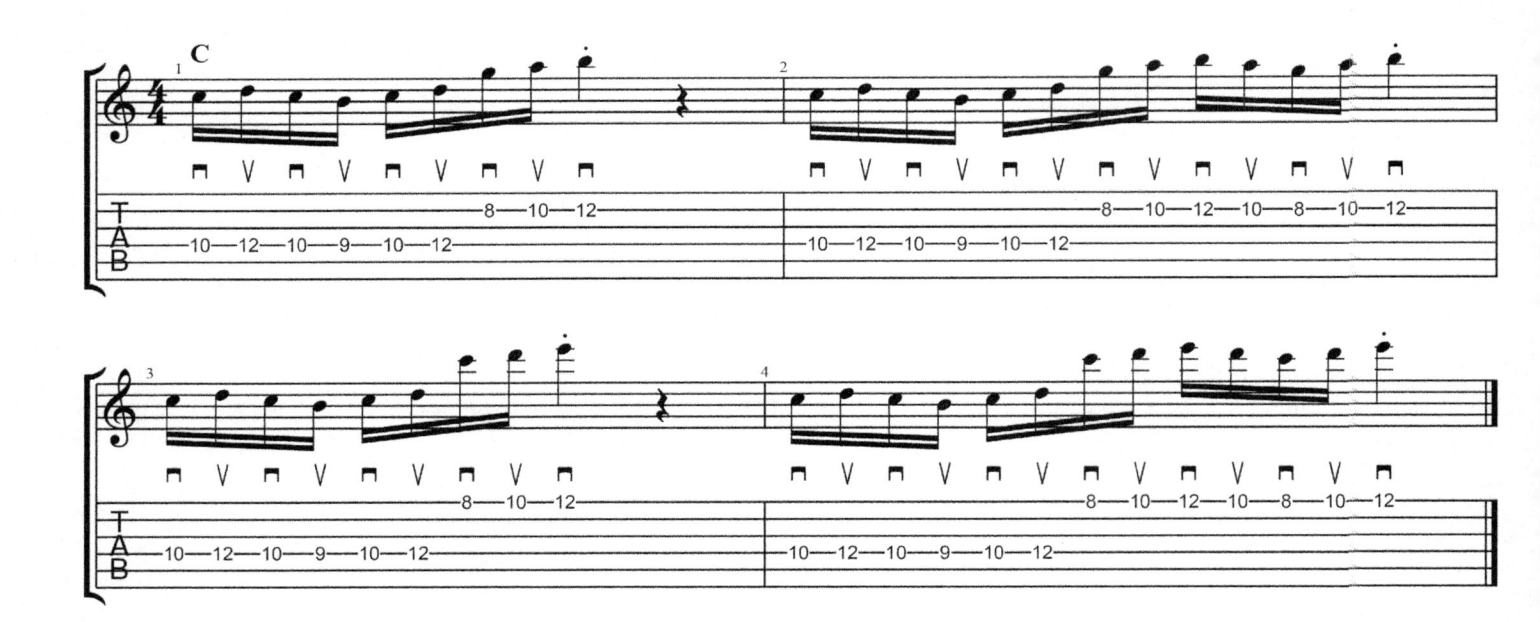

To test this kind of string change on a larger spectrum, create longer practice runs with accents to mark each new string. Even numbers are a simple way to ensure the same inside picking occurs every time.

Example 4e:

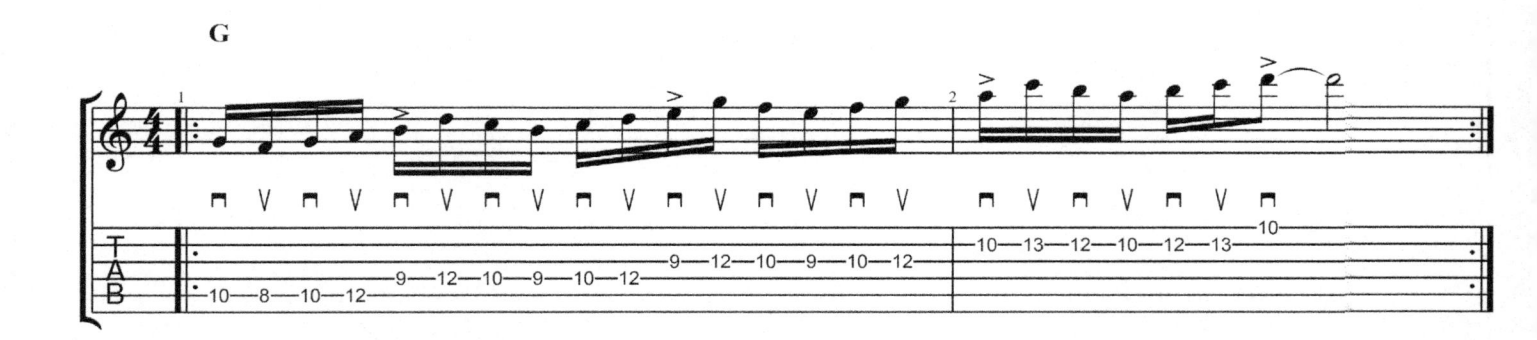

For the second kind of inside picking string change (a downstroke on a higher string followed by an upstroke on a lower string), a similar process of development and improvement works.

Watch the video to see how I manoeuvre the pick away from the strings on downstrokes to have easy access to each new string beginning on an upstroke. A consistent approach through the whole lick keeps my hands synchronized and my picking accurate.

Example 4f:

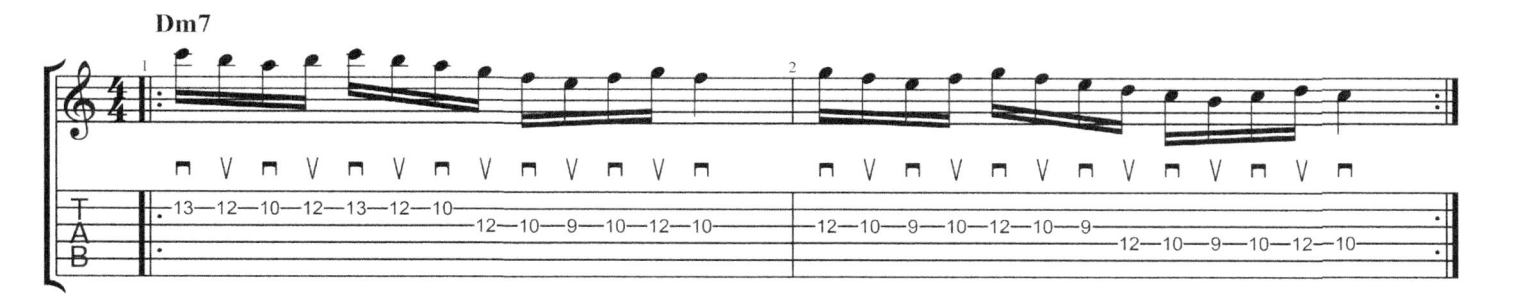

Example 4g demonstrates several stages of the isolation process, from just the string change through to re-adding notes from either side of the change.

Example 4g:

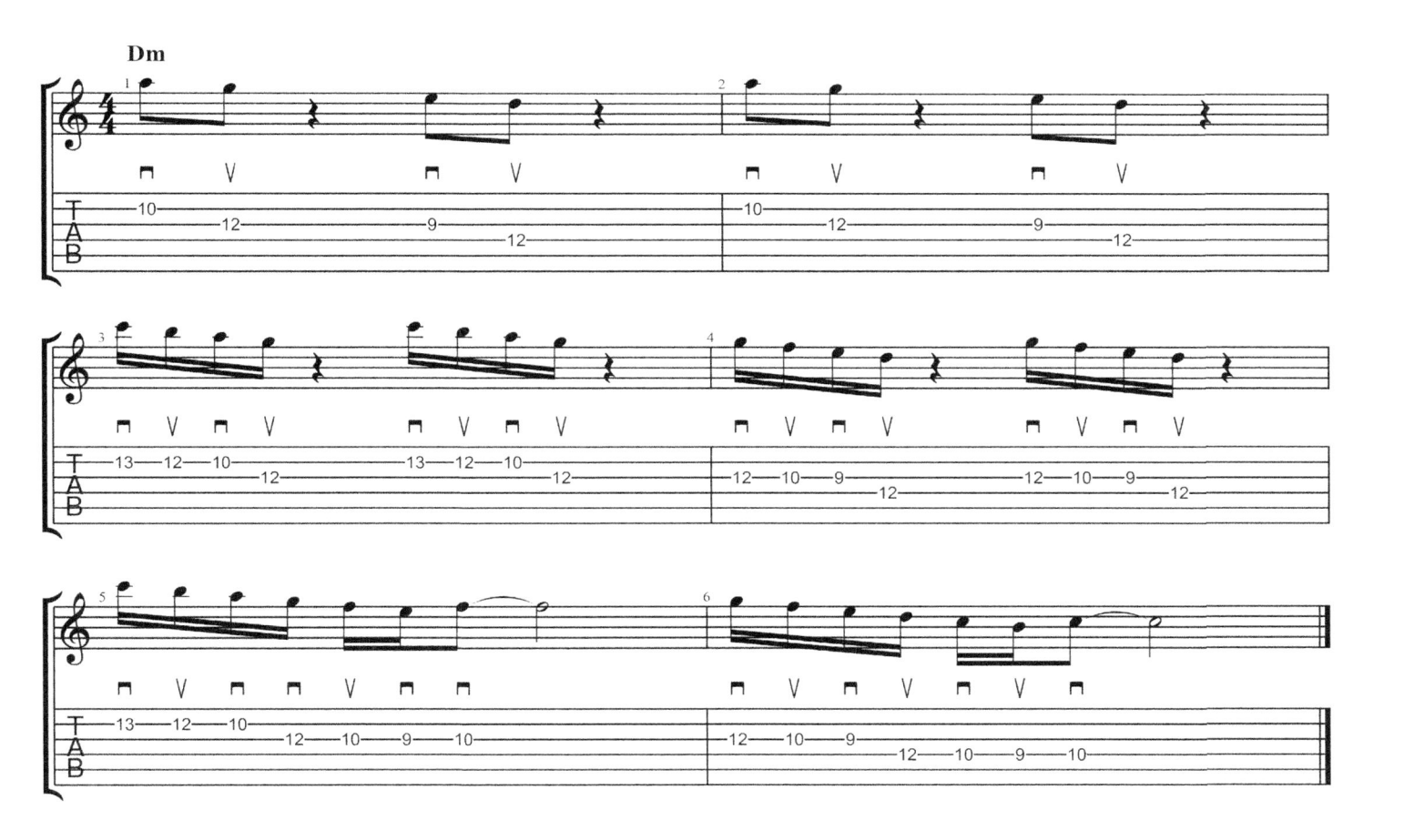

41

String-skipping will also work well here for exaggerating the distance between strings. Since we're amplifying the difficulty of the picking, pay extra close attention to the first upstroke on each lower string.

Example 4h:

For outside picking from lower strings to higher strings, try Example 4i. It is made up of a six-note figure sequenced on string pairs.

The first string change occurs right out of the gate from the A string to the D string. The pick needs to move out of the A string and above the D string to come back for the upstroke on the second note of the lick.

On the *and* of beat two, the six-note figure begins again on the 12th fret of the D string.

Example 4i:

The string changes can be isolated as follows.

Example 4j

42

To exaggerate, use string-skipping to increase the distance.

Example 4k:

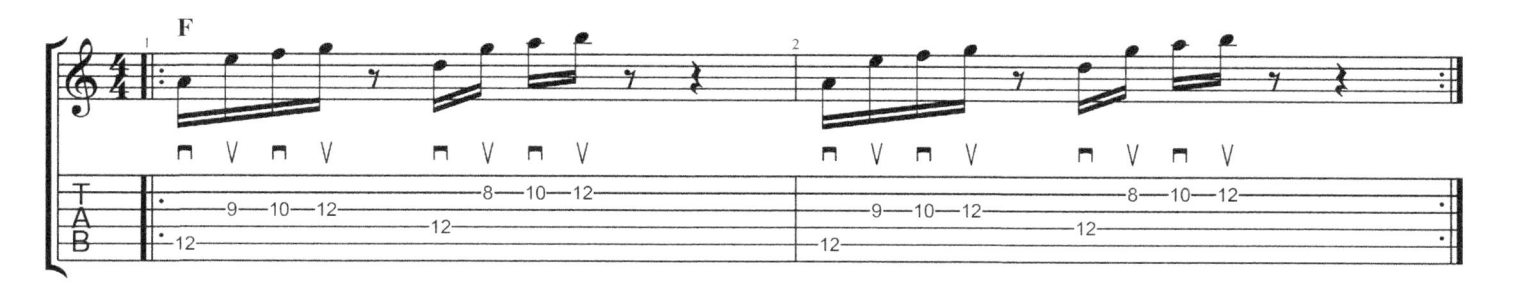

A string-skipping-exaggerated version of the picking in Example 4i might look like this.

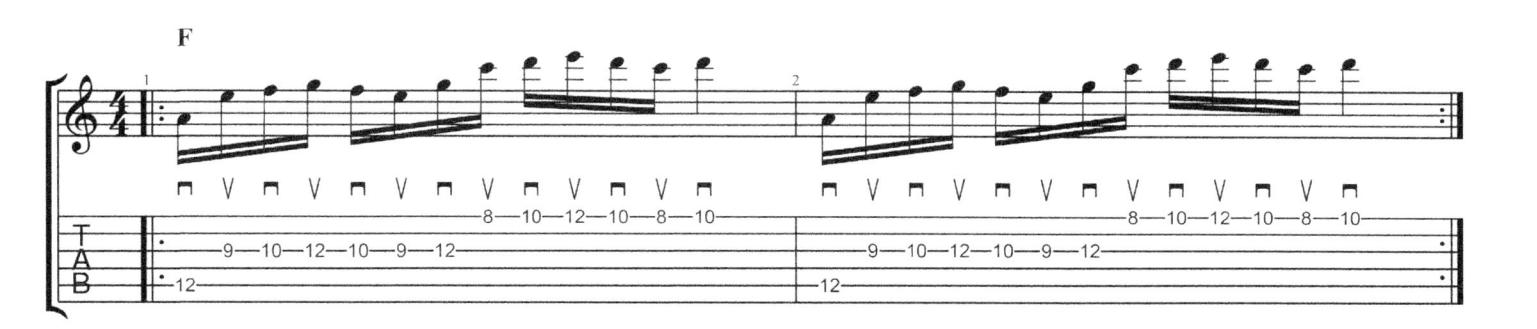

Example 4l:

The last kind of string change to address for alternate picking is an outside-picked upstroke to a lower string downstroke.

Since you already know the process, here is a practice drill (Example 4m), its accompanying string-change focused isolation drill (Example 4n) and the exaggeration exercise (Example 4o).

All three are played with the pick escaping the plane of the strings on upstrokes (see video).

Example 4m:

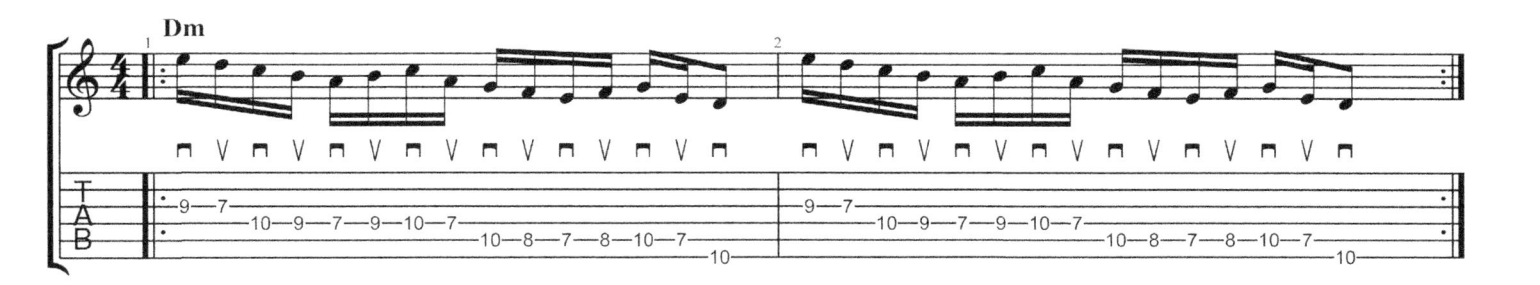

Example 4n:

Example 4o:

Playing up and down scales and sequences will undoubtedly require a mix of string changes that challenge how well you can keep it all together.

To tackle mixed string changes methodically, begin with small cells of notes and strings that provide different challenges, then apply the LIE method.

Example 4p moves up and down a one-octave C Major scale shape. The numbers above the notation indicate which string change applies.

Example 4p:

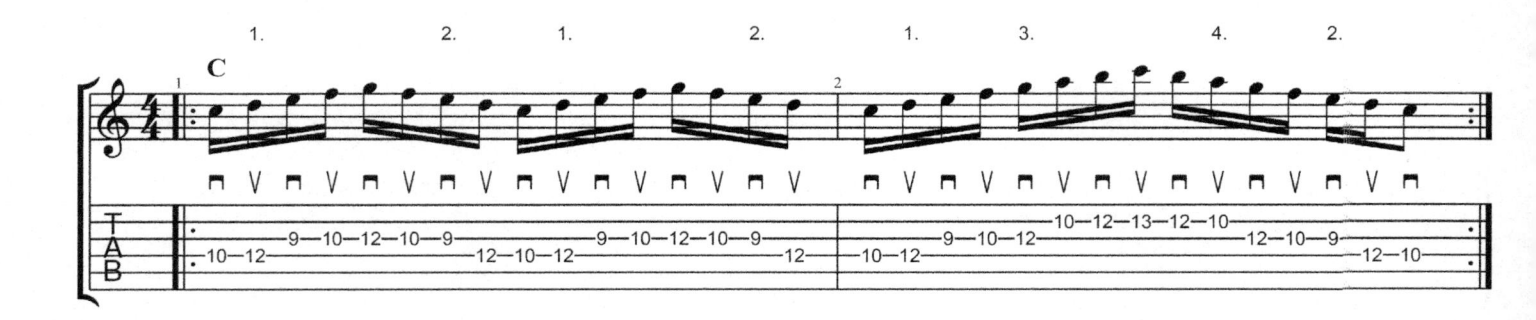

To isolate and focus on the inside picking string changes, exaggerate the number of times the string change occurs.

Example 4q:

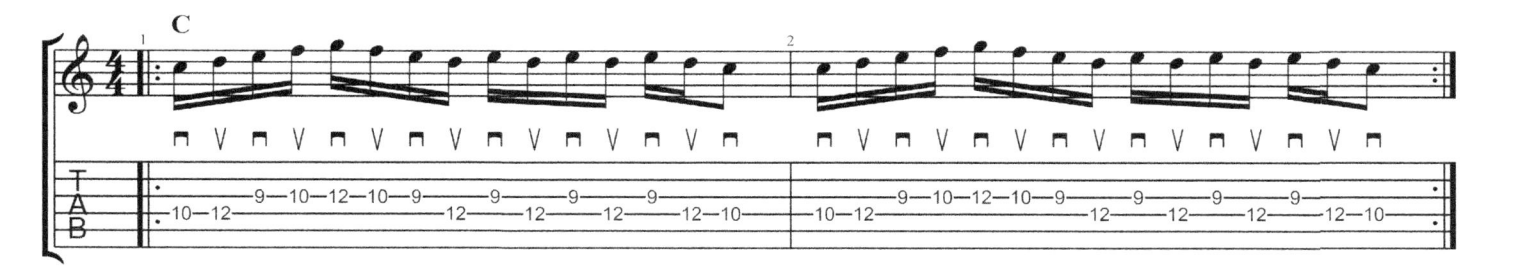

For the outside picking string changes, repetition can also be applied.

Example 4r:

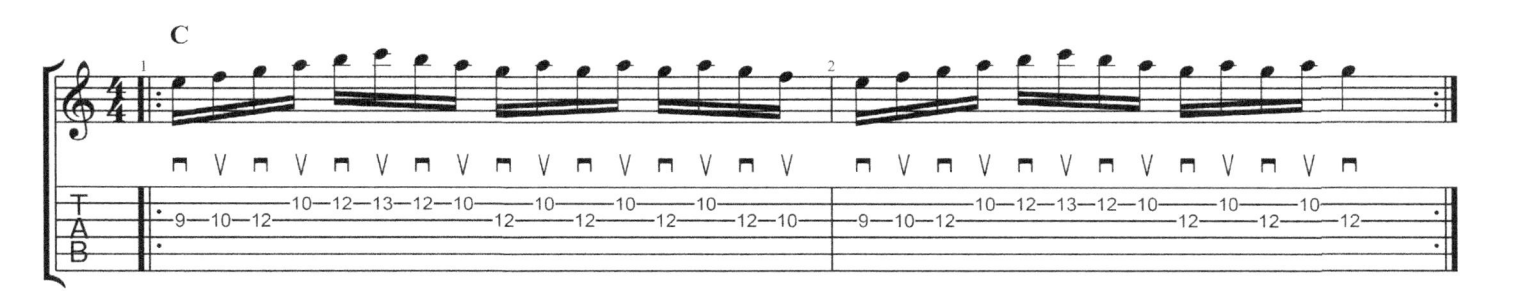

Here's an exaggeration exercise for Example 4p, beginning on the A string then moving to the G and high E strings. This will amplify any trouble you have crossing strings in time, so play with clean, accurate pick strokes.

Example 4s:

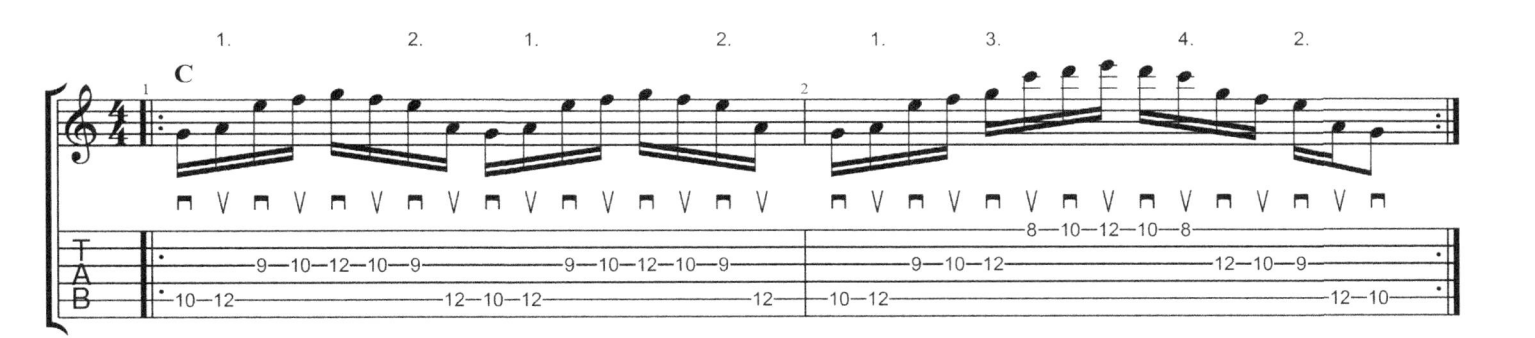

To end this chapter, I've written an etude (Example 4t) that combines alternate picking string changes with finger independence concepts from Chapter Two.

The lead line continuously draws on chromatic scale ideas but is played over a i-iv-V progression from the key of A Minor.

Each bar contains a different challenge, so isolate any bars that seem trickier than the rest and pay close attention to the fingerings to ensure you're fretting each phrase as intended.

The backing track is provided at two speeds, so give it a go once you have all the parts connected!

Example 4t:

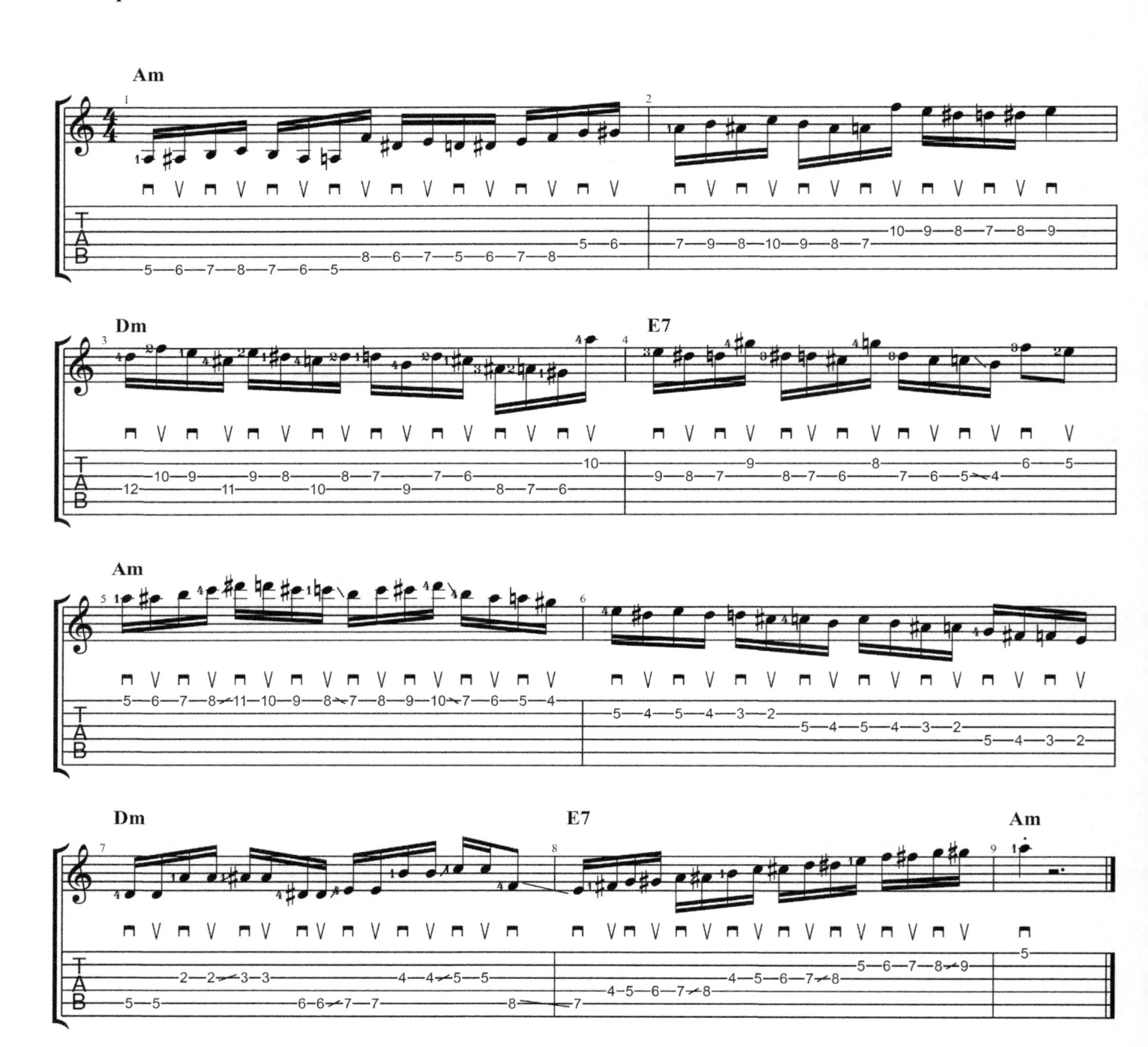

In the next chapter, we'll look at the timing and synchronization challenges of sweep and economy picking.

Chapter Five: String Crossing – Sweep and Economy Picking

Sweep and economy picking differ from alternate picking in how string changes are handled.

The two names are interchangeable and function the same way, but in guitar playing vernacular the term sweep picking is often assigned to arpeggio vocabulary, while economy picking is considered a scale-based approach.

In both, the pick takes the most direct route to each new string instead of leaping over it and doubling back (see the alternate-picked Example 4r). In many cases, the direct path from one string to another is a sweep picking motion in which one pick stroke is used for two strings and beyond.

For string changing, the synchronization and timing challenges between scales and arpeggios are similar but occur in different ratios, owing to the number of notes per string.

Since one-note-per-string arpeggios can be all sweep-picked, let's start there. For arpeggio examples, I'll be calling on major and minor triad patterns like these:

Figure 2: G Major and A Minor triads

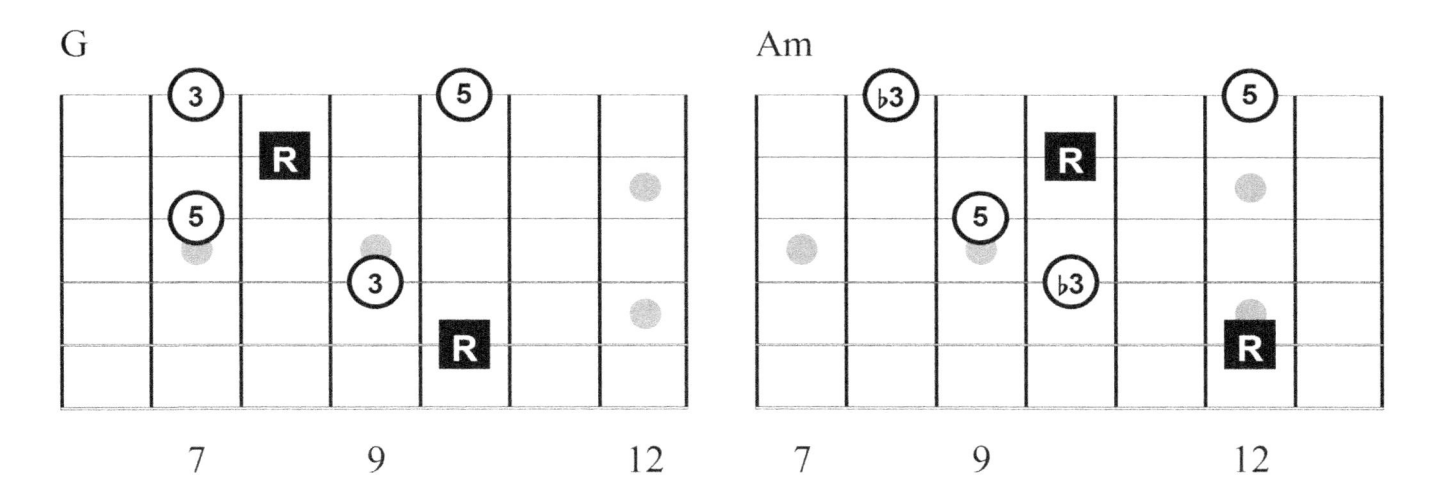

Sweep picking uses one downstroke or upstroke motion to cut through several strings in one direction. Hence, its biggest strength also opens up the possibility of unsynchronized movements between hands and the beat.

Because sweeping can seem like controlling a ball rolling down a hill at first, inexperienced sweepers risk brushing through inarticulate flurries of notes where only the first and last notes are distinguishable. Synchronization is an essential element of making sweeps sound articulate.

Let's see where you're at with sweeping using a G major triad. Take the first shape above and sweep from the A string to the high E string using one large downstroke, followed by an upstroke on the highest note.

In the video for this example, pay attention to the *rest strokes* applied by my picking hand. The pick lands on each new string straight out of the previous string, rather than in separate down motions for each note.

Example 5a:

Honesty time! Playing the previous example at your top speed, does it sound synchronized, articulate, and in time?

If not, you might have ended up with something like this: rushed, percussive in the middle, and without each finger locked into a pick stroke.

Example 5a2: Saturday morning music shop edition

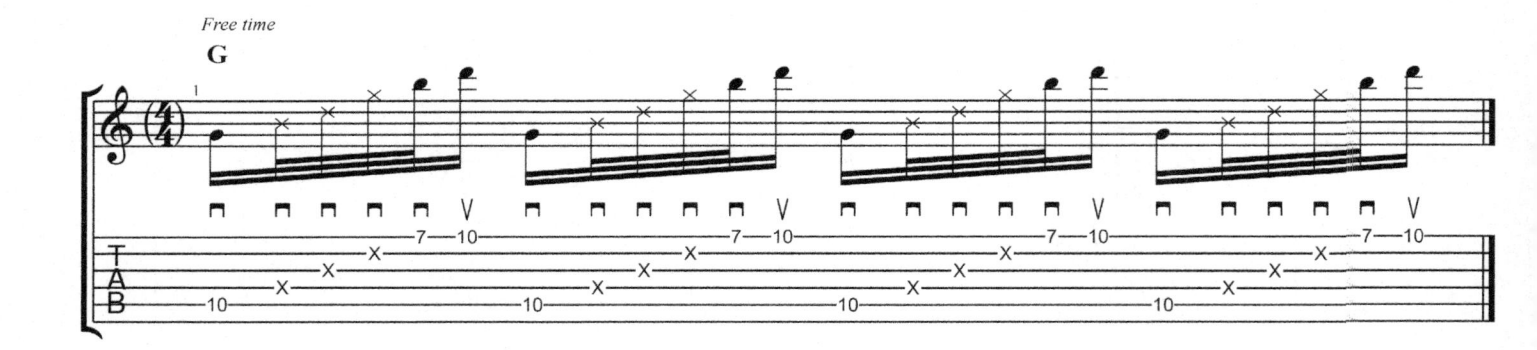

How about the descending version, where a sweeping upstroke follows one downstroke? Try this example and evaluate your timing and synchronization.

Example 5b:

If we're not careful, those swept pick strokes can get away from us, so it's beneficial to analyse sweep picking in small fragments before expanding it again.

Here are the ascending G major sweeps, broken into separate three-note ascending portions (Example 5c) and descending portions (Example 5d). Execute each group with a solid sense of time, ensuring each pick stroke is paired with a fretting hand finger.

When you've worked these examples through various metronome speeds (along with foot tapping), revisit Example 5a to see if it has improved.

Example 5c:

Example 5d:

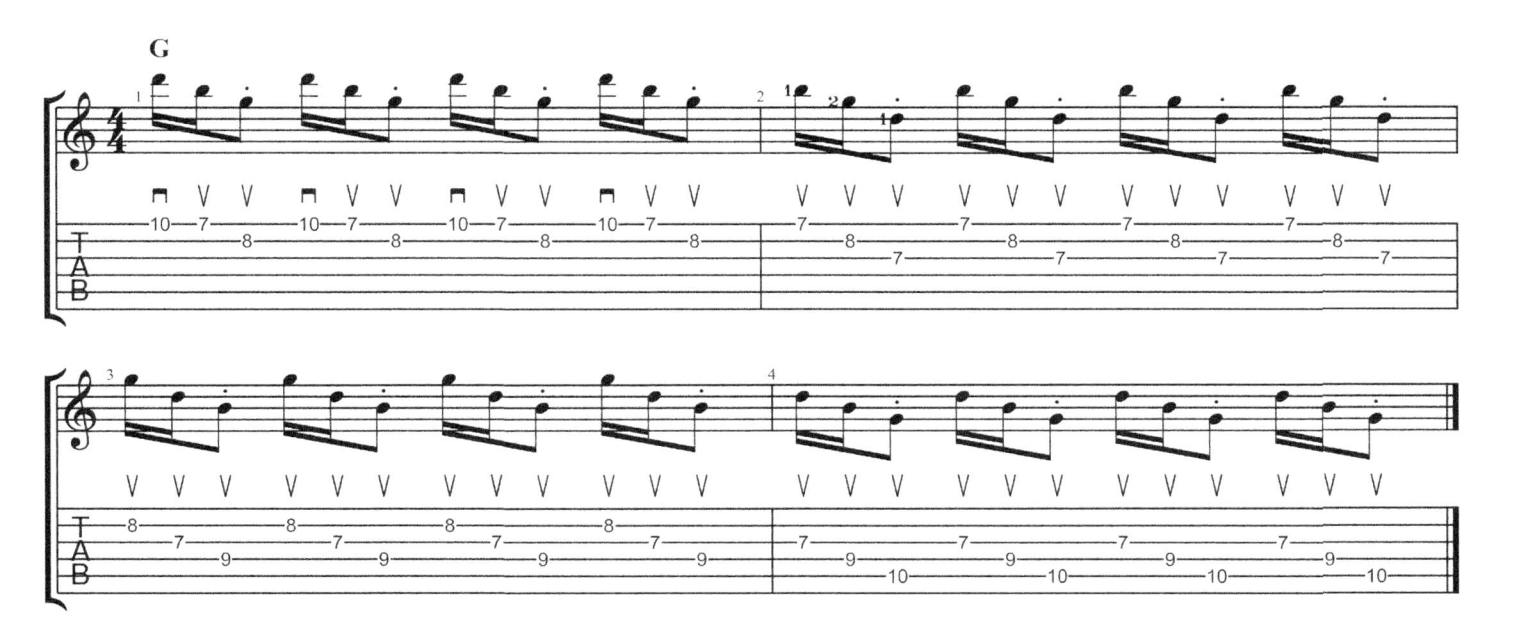

Using the minor triad shape from Figure 2, combine ascending and descending sweeps. To lock the picking hand into this example's 1/8th note triplet rhythms, begin accenting where indicated. As you speed up, you can limit the accents to the first note of each direction.

Example 5e:

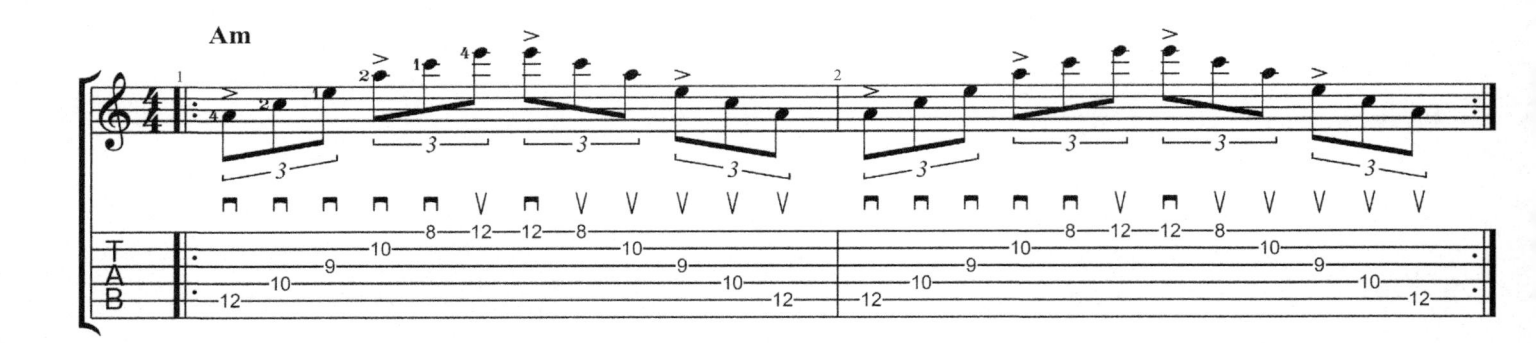

To nail position slides between arpeggios, they can be isolated for synchronization focus, then played right through, as demonstrated in Example 5f.

Example 5f:

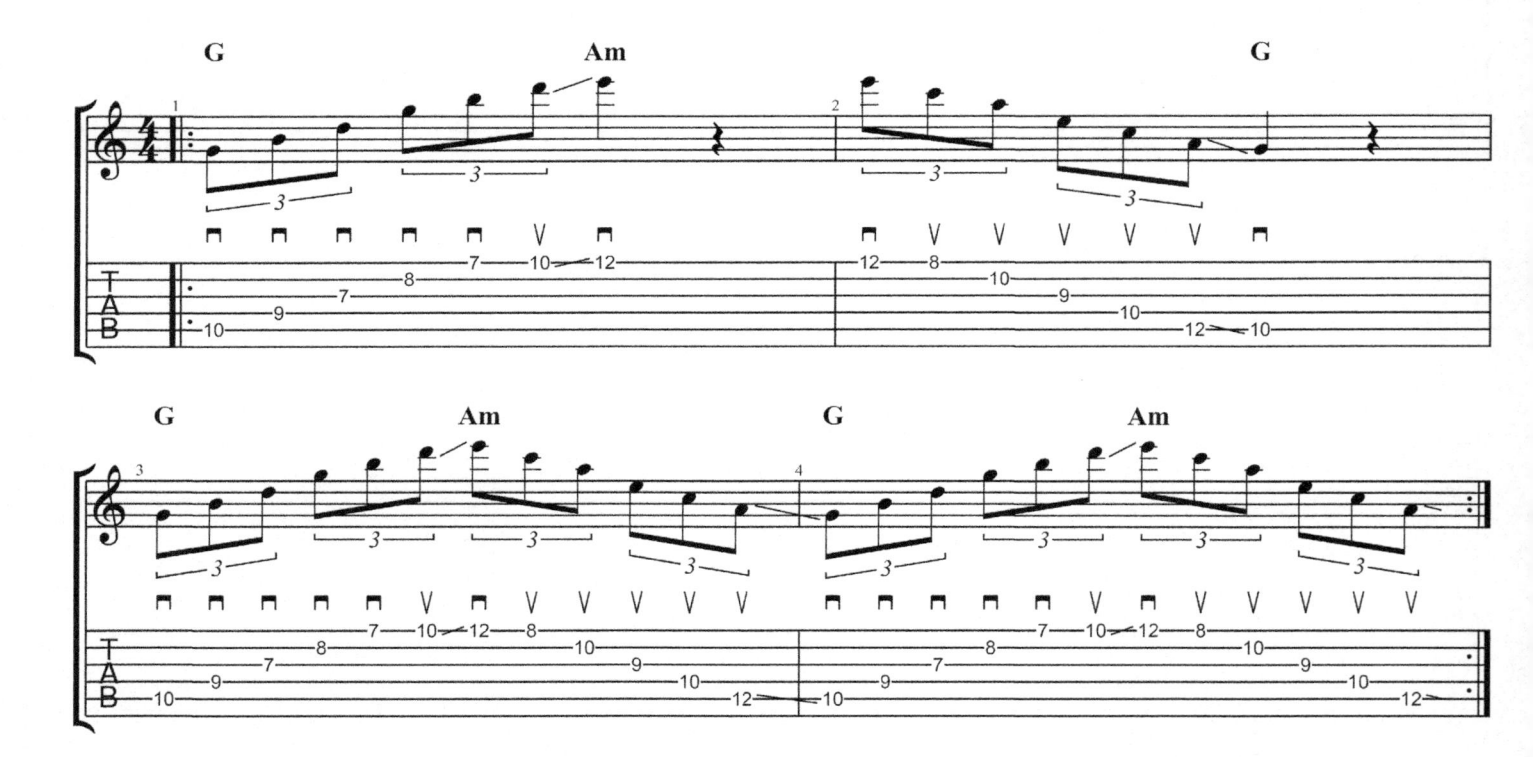

The challenge of well-timed, synchronized economy picking for scale lines is slightly different. Rather than the pick moving to multiple strings in quick succession like an arpeggio, scale playing contains alternate picking along each string between string changes.

In Example 5g, a downstroke begins each ascending string, and an upstroke begins each descending string. The pick sweeps each change and never needs to escape the plane of the strings.

Example 5g:

To improve the timing of the previous example, string changes can be isolated and repeated like this:

Example 5h:

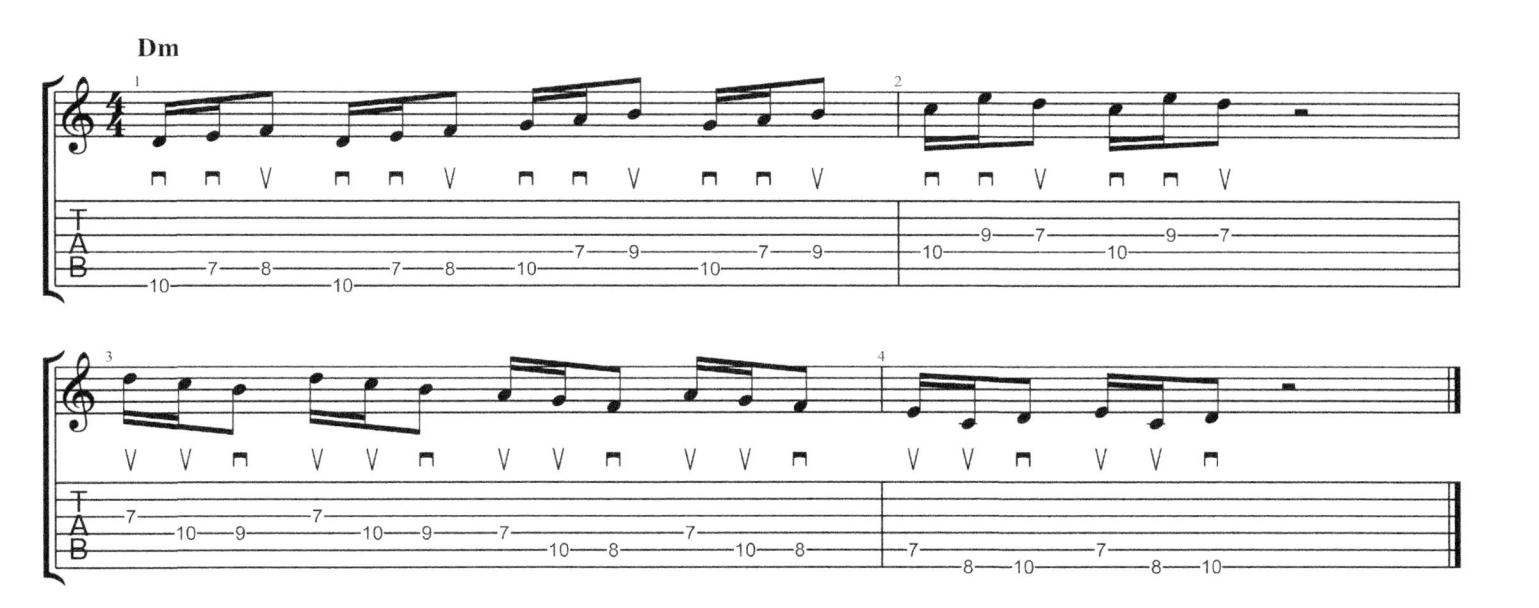

When the string changes have improved, go back to the original line in Example 5g. This time, think less about the string changes and put heavy accents on the beats to bring things back to being about timing.

In the video, note how I lean the pick in the direction I'm travelling, decreasing resistance on the pick.

Example 5i (Example 5g with accents):

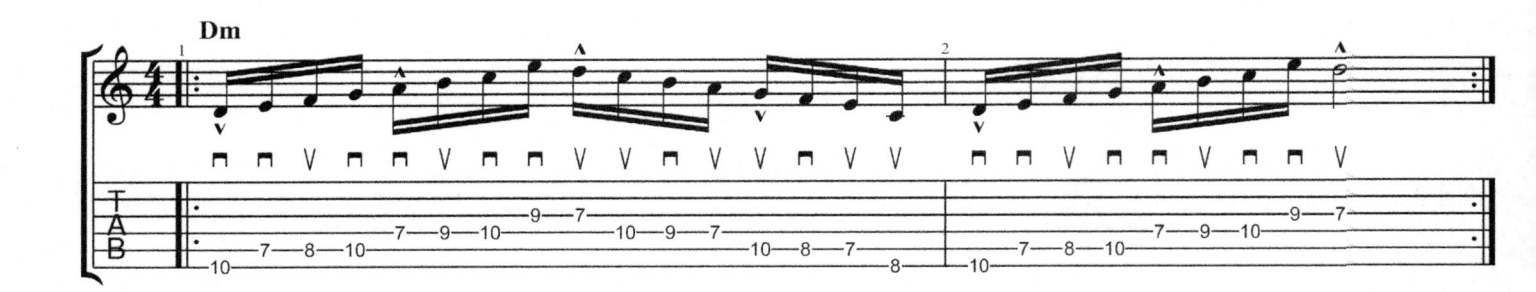

[Notation and tablature in Dm, 4/4 time]

The final aspect of economy picking string-crossing timing is the placement of string changes to the beat.

With three-note-per-string scales, it's easy to get comfortable with sweeping into a new string on a beat, but it can be trickier when the phrasing doesn't align.

Here's an example of string changes occurring on beats 1, 2, and 3 in each bar.

Example 5j:

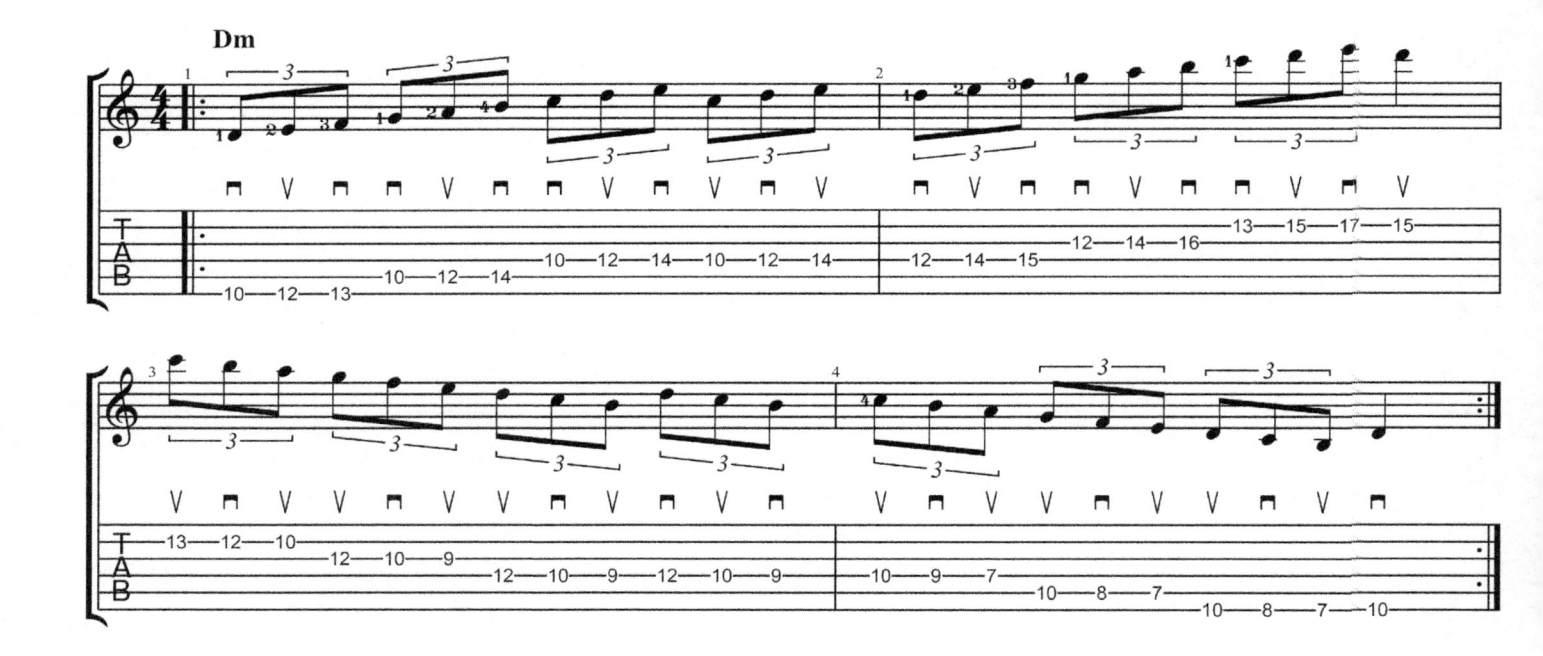

[Notation and tablature in Dm, 4/4 time]

Using the same notes in 1/16th note subdivisions takes a little more focus, so commit the previous phrase to memory and change your focus to playing steady groups of four.

Example 5k:

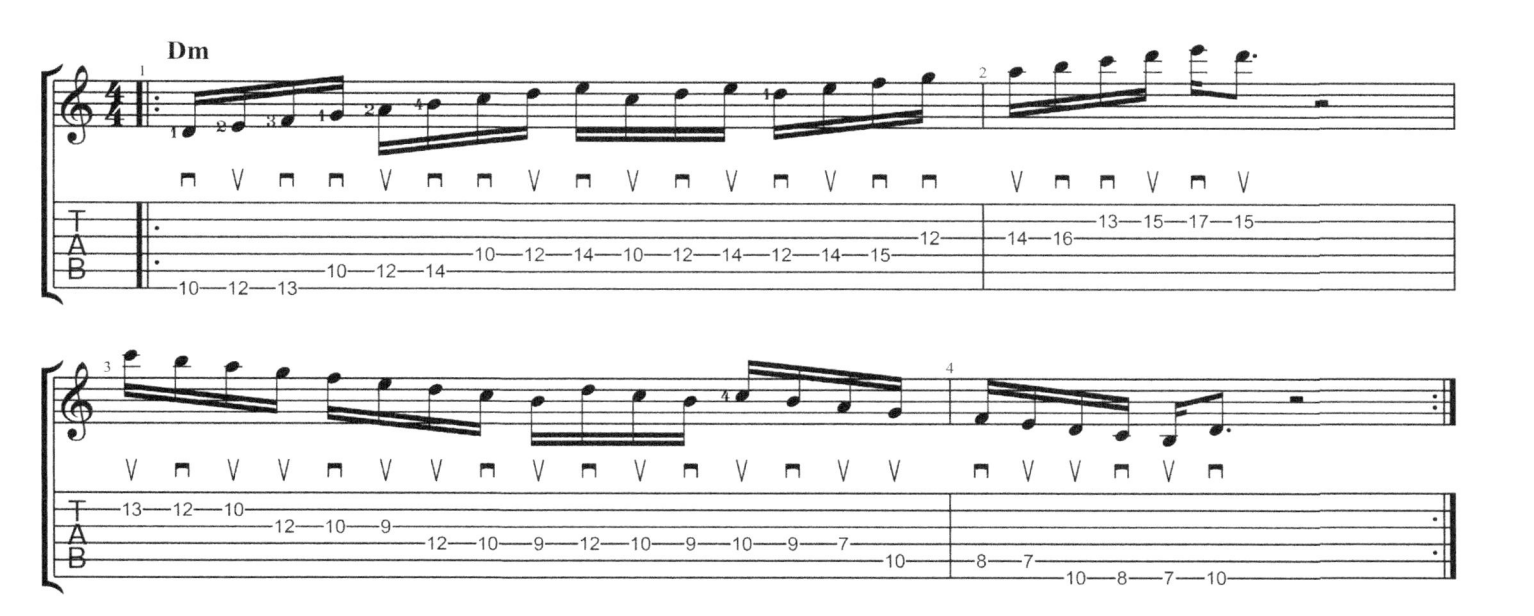

In one last version of the same picking line, Example 5l is phrased in sextuplets. Some string changes occur on the beat, while others happen halfway through.

Mechanically, there's no difference in playing the lick, so your focus on synchronizing to the beat is the only variable.

Example 5l:

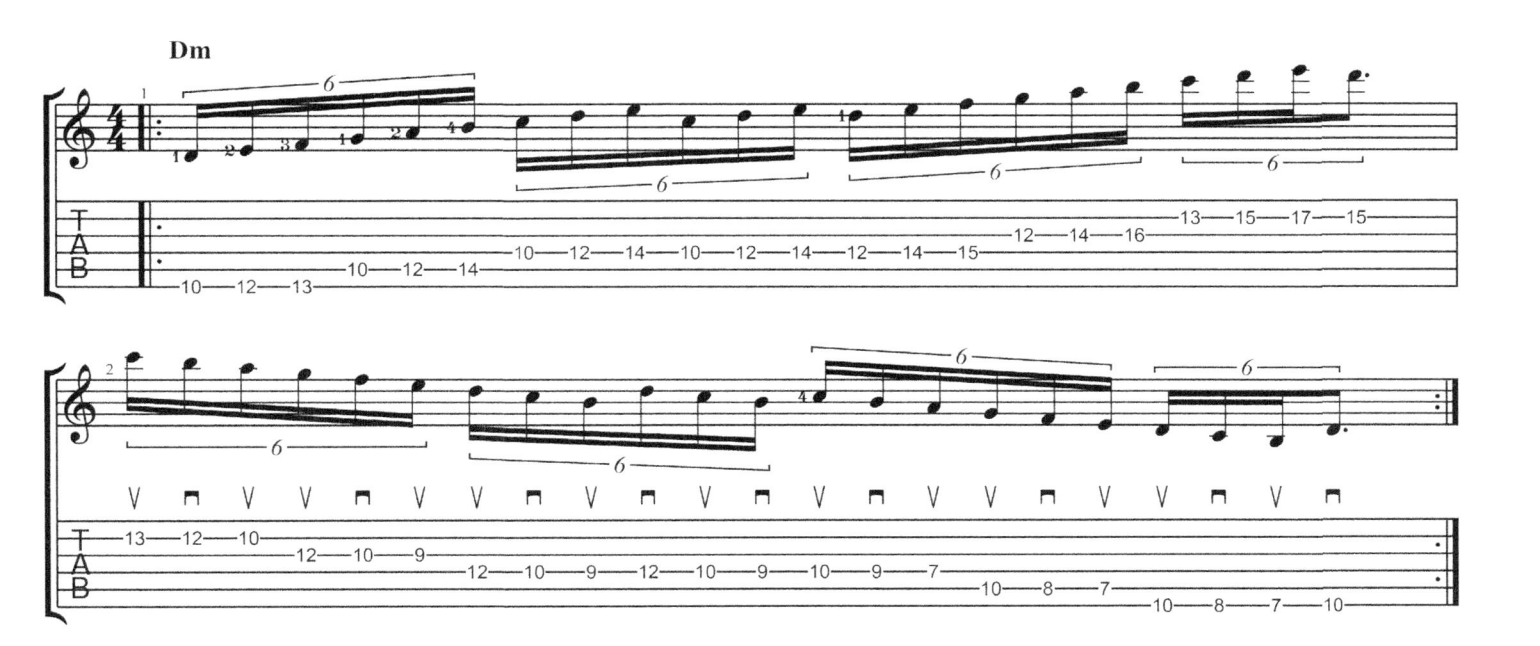

53

To improve synchronization on sweep and economy picked lines, keep the following in mind:
- Focus on playing arpeggios in steady time before you try breaking any Guinness records
- Each finger should be in-sync with its relevant pick stroke
- Arpeggios can be broken up into smaller pieces for timing practice
- Economy picking scales will combine single string alternate picking with sweeping
- Isolating string changes allows more significant focus on string-change timing
- It's crucial to work on string changes that don't always coincide with the beat

Chapter Six: Legato and Picking Interplay

Legato, meaning "tied together" in Italian, is mainly considered a fretting hand technique in guitar-speak.

Hammer-ons, pull-offs, and slides are used to connect notes on the fretboard to create smoother-sounding lines than the bolder attack of constant picking.

This chapter will expand on fretting hand timing, touched on in Chapter One, and move into the role of the pick in extended legato licks and the synchronization required between the hands.

Let's start with a quick comparison between picked notes and slurs.

Where picking offers a steady way to lock into the beat (bar one), legato articulates notes from finger to finger (bar two) using slurs (ascending: hammer-ons, descending: pull-offs).

Example 6a:

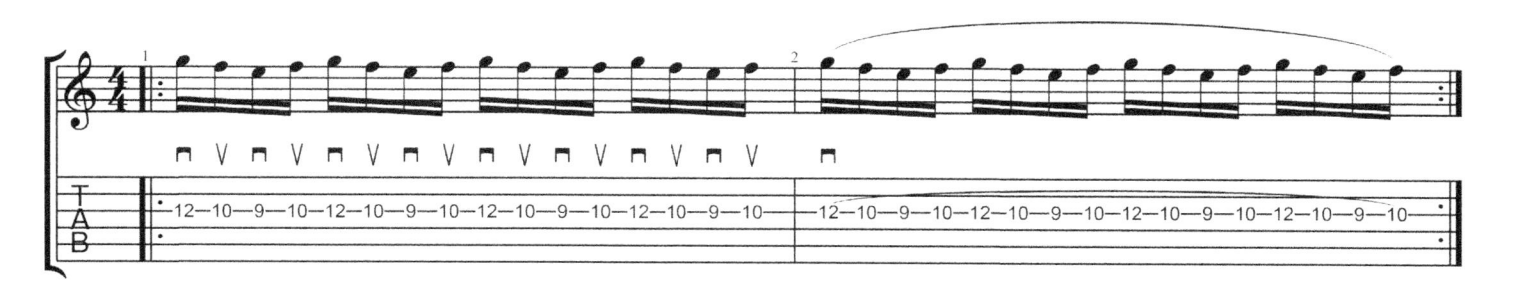

In the second bar of the previous example, the fingers must work harder than simply holding the notes down for the picking hand to articulate. Each hammer-on and pull-off needs to be audible and in time.

Here's a way to slow down, pay attention to each slur, and then increase the frequency and speed within one example. Since there's no picking hand to lock into, try nodding your head to the beat, along with your tapping foot, for an emphasis on internal rhythm.

Example 6b:

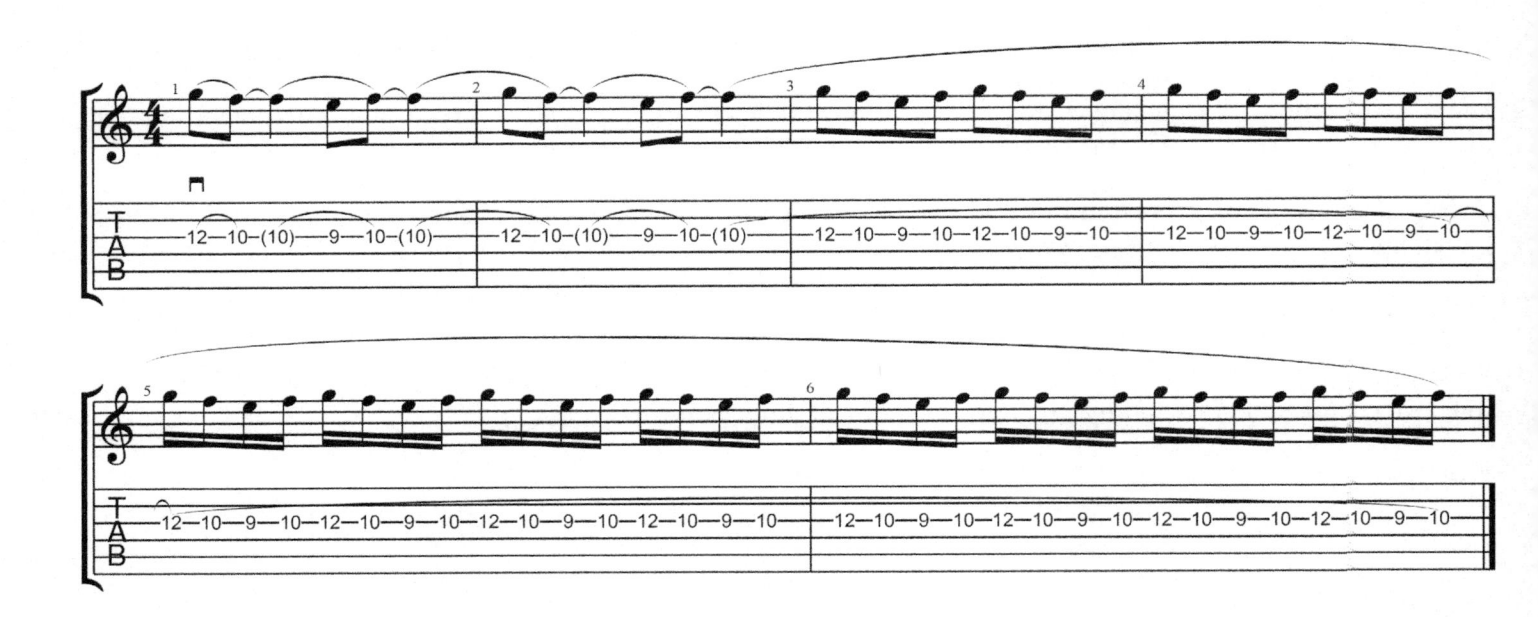

Using a new six-note figure, Example 6c moves down the G string in every configuration of semitone and whole tone note spacings, comparing legato in bars one and two to the picking in bars three and four.

Aim to get both halves of the exercise equally locked into the beat.

Example 6c:

The timing of slides is also an essential aspect of legato playing. The following sequence uses whole tone and semitone slides according to the key without the benefit of a pick to steady the timing.

Example 6d:

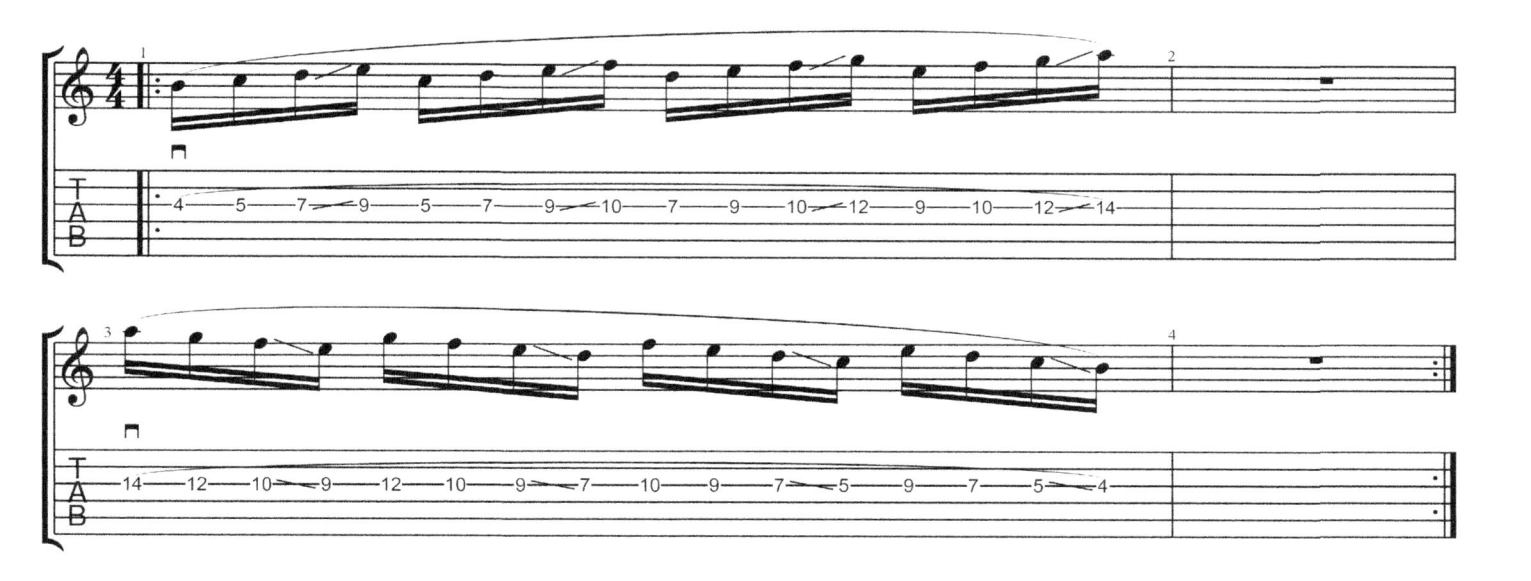

[Musical notation and tablature showing:
Measure 1: 4-5-7-9-5-7-9-10-7-9-10-12-9-10-12-14
Measure 3: 14-12-10-9-12-10-9-7-10-9-7-5-9-7-5-4]

To work on slide timing in stages, try this 1/8th note version. After you've spent some time on this example, return to Example 6d.

Example 6e:

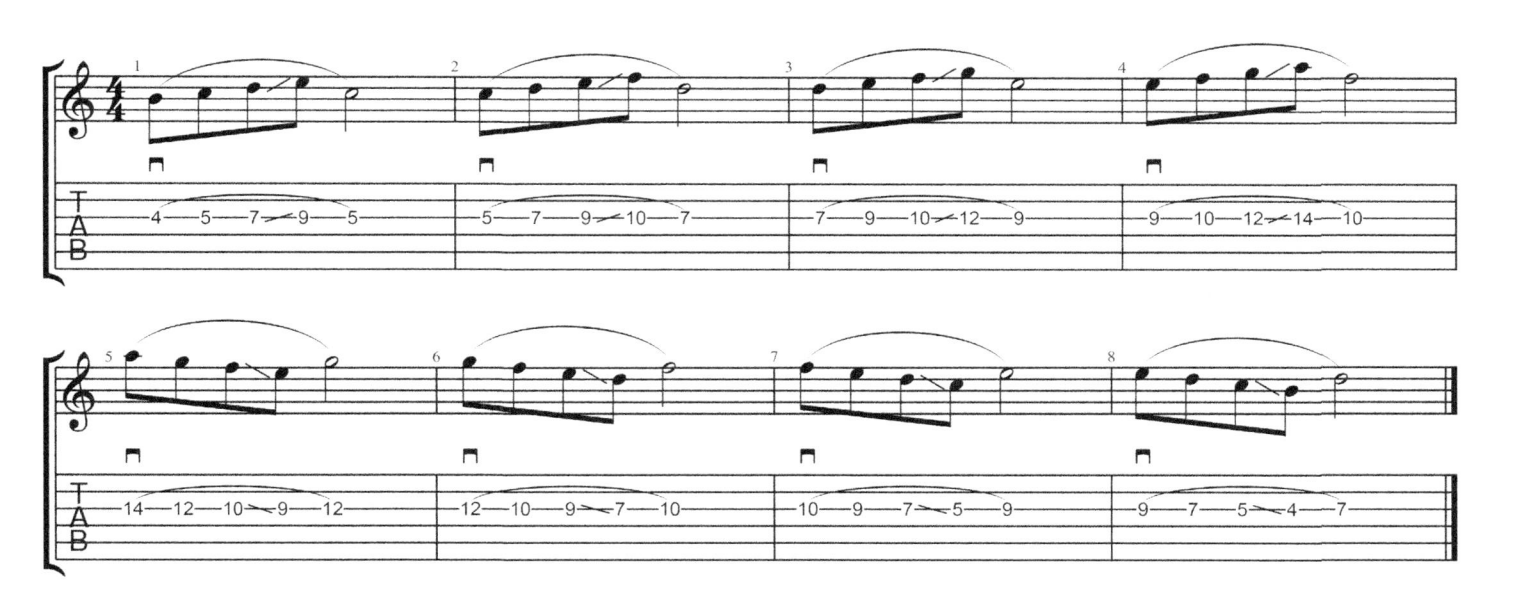

[Musical notation and tablature showing:
Measure 1: 4-5-7-9-5
Measure 2: 5-7-9-10-7
Measure 3: 7-9-10-12-9
Measure 4: 9-10-12-14-10
Measure 5: 14-12-10-9-12
Measure 6: 12-10-9-7-10
Measure 7: 10-9-7-5-9
Measure 8: 9-7-5-4-7]

There are several options for initiating multiple strings in legato licks to get things moving on each string. Consider this Paul Gilbert-style legato drill, where each string begins with a pick stroke.

Gilbert likes to work on the outside of the strings, thinking in terms of *up/down* from the high E string to the B string and *down/up* from the G string to the B string.

Example 6f:

Let's look at three other options.

First, we'll try inside picking on every string change (Example 6g), then maximise sweep picking opportunities in two directions (Example 6h) and, finally, use the pick for ascending strings only (Example 6i).

Try each and determine your personal preference.

Example 6g:

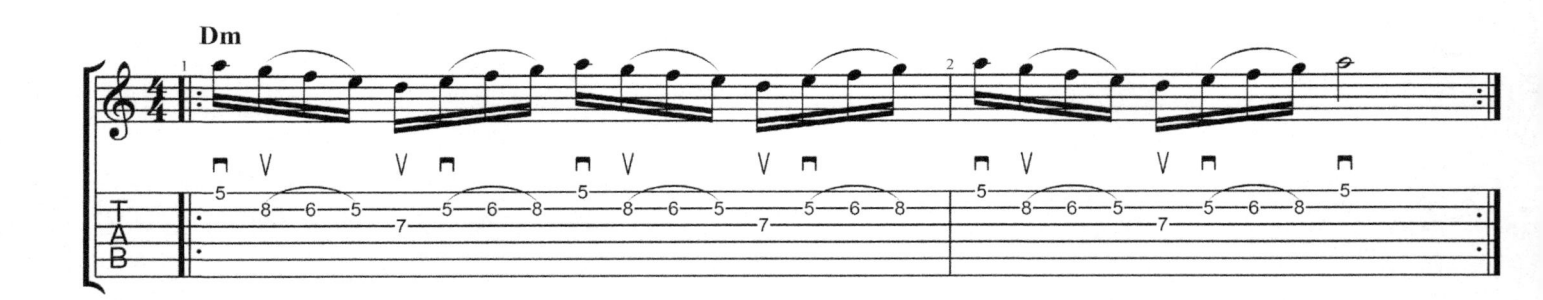

Example 6h:

Example 6i:

Test the timing of your preferred approach by isolating the picking elements.

For comparison, Example 6j is a drill that switches from the outside picking of Example 6f to the sweep approach of Example 6g.

Muting the strings with the fretting hand and working percussively is a great way to listen to the timing of the pick strokes in relation to the metronome beat.

If you hear any rushing or dragging, slow down, exaggerate the pick strokes by using more force to emphasise the rhythm, then speed up again to see if you've eliminated the timing issue.

Example 6j:

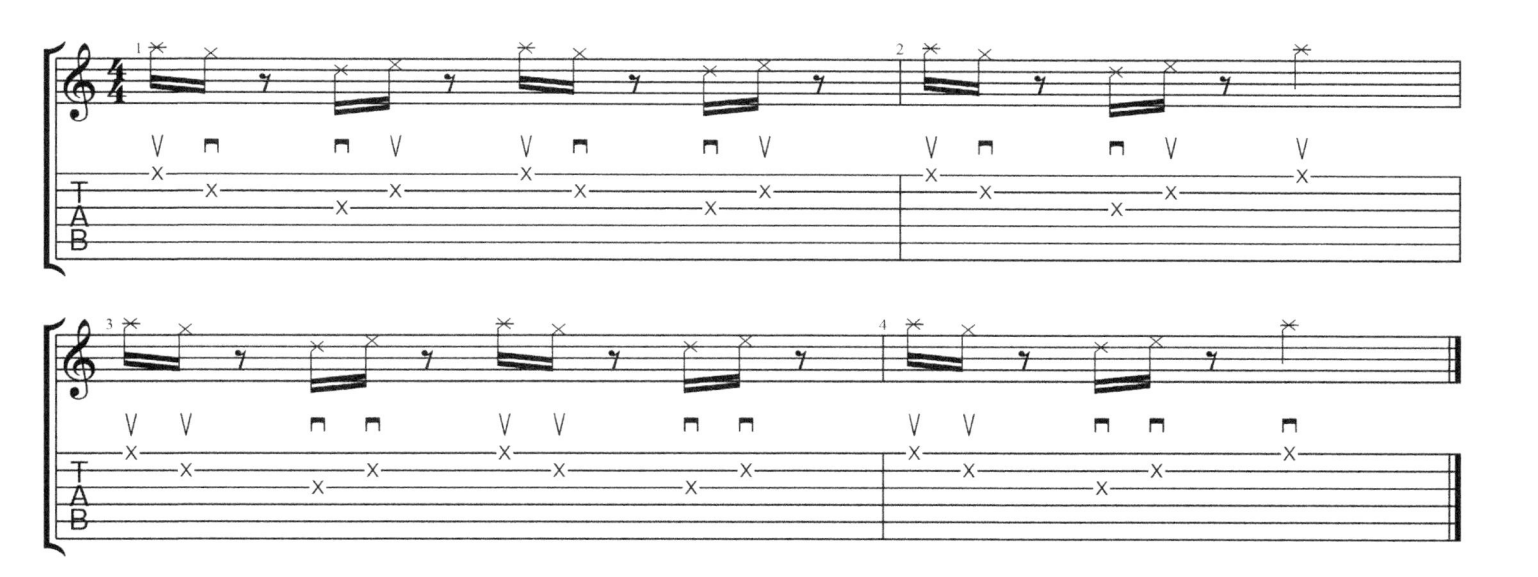

Here's a more extended comparison of outside picking string changes (bar one) and inside picking (bar two). Determine a preference and make that your go-to approach.

59

Example 6k:

To use exaggeration as an improvement tool for picking and legato licks, let's revisit the idea of string skipping to make fretting and picking jumps between strings wider.

This lick is a more challenging version of the Paul Gilbert style idea of Example 6f.

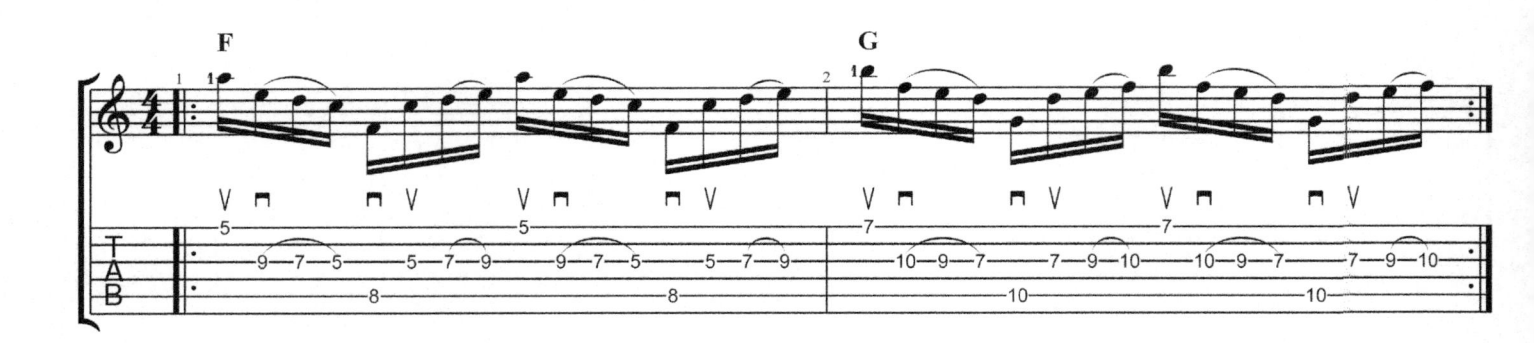

Example 6l:

To test the synchronization of your chosen picking type across all strings, here's a four-bar descending run that works over an A minor chord or A power chord.

The pick strokes indicated reflect an outside picking preference. To use inside picking, reverse every pick stroke except for the final upstroke in bar four.

Example 6m:

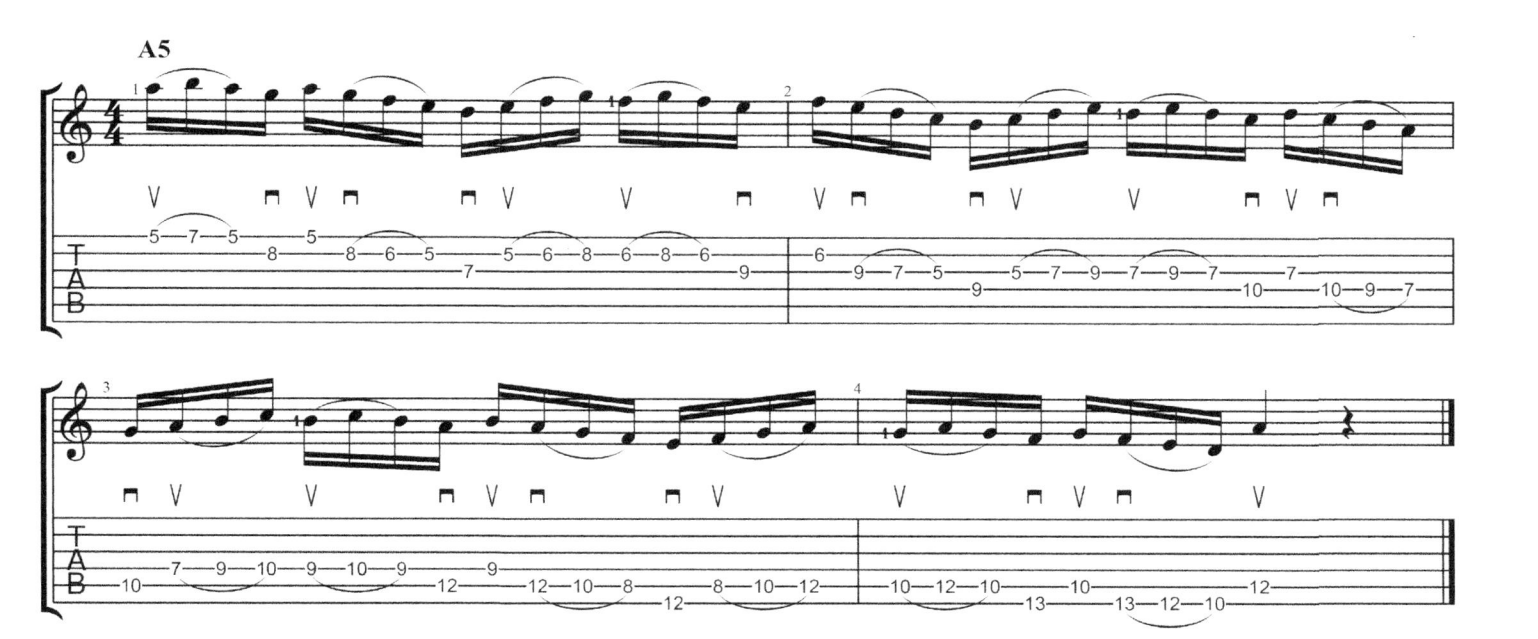

To perfect the timing and synchronization of any legato lick you work on, address the following:

- The rhythm of the lick, i.e., 1/16th notes, 1/8th note triplets etc
- Which fingers fall on the beats of the bar
- Where the string changes occur and how you'll execute them
- The overall timing of the lick at comfortable speeds
- Any problems that arise as you speed up. Locate, isolate, and exaggerate to overcome them.

Section One Summary

Throughout the chapters of this section, we've covered a range of practical tools for playing better guitar, laying the foundations to move ahead with speed in Section Two.

You're better positioned to take it to new levels as you read ahead by improving your timing, synchronization, and general facility on the instrument.

Here's a list of what you've accomplished in Section One:

- Improving inner timing by learning to lock your body into the beat
- Dividing the beat into various subdivisions with the pick while staying in time
- Timing the placement of the fretting hand fingers
- Synchronizing the hands to work as one cohesive unit
- Finding challenging fingerings and overcoming them with focused drills
- Playing chromatic and diatonic drills to reinforce good habits
- Locating, isolating, and exaggerating challenges to rise above them
- String changing using alternate picking, sweep/economy picking, and legato
- Accumulated 90 exercises to draw upon for practice

I'll give you the tools to play faster and more economically in Section Two.

Section Two: Speeding Up

"If you want something you have never had, you must be willing to do something you have never done". – often attributed to Thomas Jefferson.

The quote might not be a saying of Jefferson's, but it does offer some insight into development.

Growth happens outside the comfort zone, and achieving new things is often facilitated by a new mindset.

We've all heard well-meaning advice for getting faster at the guitar. Frequently offered tips include:

- Practice slow to get fast
- Speed occurs through repetition
- You only need small motions
- You should always practice with a metronome
- Increase the metronome tempo a few bpm at a time to become fast
- It needs to be perfect before it can be fast

Some of the above have merit for developing motor skills, playing in time, and aiming for quality – all great attributes for your playing. You've already followed several of these processes to get to this point in the book.

But to develop one's potential for speed, speed must be examined as a separate pursuit. If all of the above tips were self-fulfilling for speed development, everyone who plays neatly to a metronome would be as fast as they want.

Some studies have even shown that mindlessly repeating the same thing can benefit less than the concepts in this section.

If you've tried all of the above and cannot play at the speed you'd like, you already know that there's more to the picture. A new approach is required.

In this section, I will walk you through the steps to aim higher and play faster using a system I formulated in my practice routines three decades ago.

As a teenager, I went from barely knowing when to use an upstroke to playing my favourite speed licks from videos by Paul Gilbert and Vinnie Moore in less than two years, and that's while I was still figuring out my practice approach.

Dropping it all here for you to study, I believe you'll get results in a fraction of the time it took me.

Before we grab the keys to the Lamborghini and hit the accelerator, it's crucial to create a tension-free guitar experience.

Chapter Seven covers playing in a relaxed manner to avoid injury, economise effort and maximise your results for the rest of the book.

Chapter Seven: Playing Without Tension

Tension, the muscular kind, is the enemy of speed, fluidity, and – even worse – longevity as a player if it leads to injury. Playing in a way that fosters pain has no payoff. It's all bad news.

Muscle tension is different from using your technique to create dynamics, aggression, accents, etc. All of these can be achieved in a mechanically responsible way without the escalating accumulation of aches, pains, and discomfort that tension results in.

When raising this subject in countless lessons over the years, I joked with students that the two-step process for playing without tension is:

1. Start without any
2. Keep it that way

As unhelpful as the gag sounds, it raises the point of habit. Many players who have developed tension did so through repetition. Something was played with too much tension, then again and again, until playing tensely became the default response.

Conversely, many legendary players who play blazing lines are lauded for how effortless they make it look.

The great news is that good and bad habits develop the same way – one repeat at a time. Correcting your technique might be frustrating, but keep in mind that every correct repeat of a movement brings you closer to *that* being your body's default response.

Occasionally, you'll slip back into your old ways, but the more correct repeats you add to your scorecard, the more likely you will make good default decisions. Call yourself out when you notice too much tension, then start again.

There is a changeover period when doing something incorrectly might feel more familiar than doing it correctly, but that is the improvement process. Just like the clay in a pottery class, your good habits need to bake long enough in the kiln to make them permanent and harder to break.

Any advice here is offered as a guitarist, not a doctor. Please seek professional advice and treatment options if you're already experiencing temporary or long-term pain from playing the guitar.

So, now that I think I've dodged all potential lawsuits, let's proceed.

My checklist is the same whether you approach this topic from a preventative or corrective perspective.

The areas I like to address in reducing/preventing tension are:

- Posture and positioning of the guitar
- Fretting hand pressure
- Picking hand attack
- Picking dynamics with sustainable mechanics
- Disconnecting tension and tempo

Posture and Position

My priority for setting up the positioning of the guitar is to do so in a way that allows the guitar to sit comfortably and ergonomically. I want my hands to be playing the guitar, not holding it up.

The first thing I do to set up my posture is to sit straight in a chair that allows my feet to rest flat on the floor with my knees bent at ninety degrees. I don't even want my calf muscles to get tense.

I rest my guitar in what many call the classical position on my left (non-dominant side) leg and use a footstool under that foot. As formal as it sounds, this positioning allows my guitar to sit perfectly and be ready for playing – even without a strap or before I rest my forearm on the guitar's body.

My strap length is adjusted to have very little slack in the seated position. I can stand up and have the guitar in a similar position, which removes any issue of not being able to stand up to play things I have practiced sitting down. It doesn't make me look as cool as Slash, but it provides consistency.

Figure 3:

Resting the guitar on your dominant leg is fine too, if you can sustain hours of playing in that position. After many years of that approach, I found myself twisting my body and not keeping my shoulders level when I wasn't playing the guitar.

If you have felt a bit twisted in the "rock position" or that your guitar is not fully supported, try the classical position and see how it feels.

Fretting Hand Pressure

Now that your guitar is sitting securely and you're not using your hands to hold it, let's consider fretting hand pressure.

Remember the first open chord you ever learned, or the first note you had to press down? It felt like it took all the strength you could muster to bring the strings down to the point where they made a sound.

Over time, you proved that those first few challenges weren't as complex as they seemed. You built a little finger strength, improved your technique, started fretting just behind the fret wire, and so on.

As a more experienced player, it's time to challenge what you might currently be doing out of habit, including how hard you press down strings in your scale and lead playing.

If you have felt your fretting arm getting tense (fingers, wrist, forearm etc.,) here's a simple retraining exercise.

With your thumb in a supportive position behind the neck, use your index finger to contact the B string at the 5th fret, without pressing down.

You'll hear a percussive sound from the muted string when you pick. Gradually bring your index finger down to the fretboard throughout several pick strokes until you hear a clear note. Hold that for a moment with the very little pressure it took to sound the note, then repeat from "choked" to a clear sound again.

Example 7a:

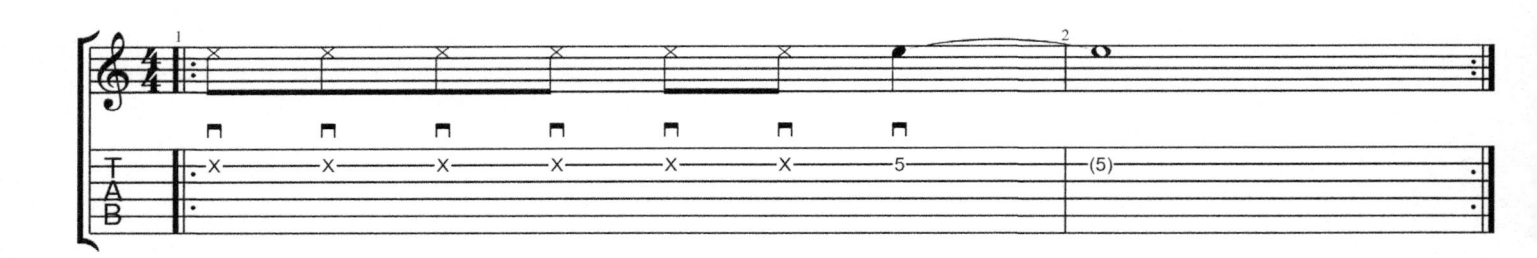

Follow the same process for each finger: starting with no pressure and stopping when you hear a clear note.

Example 7b:

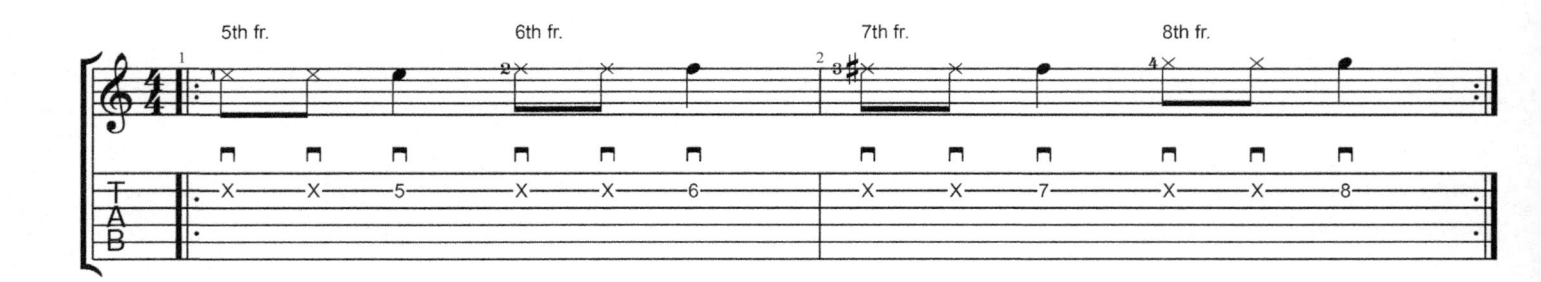

Play each of the clear notes now using only the amount of pressure you applied for the final note of each finger in Example 7b. For the sake of the exercise, only the finger being used should contact the string.

Example 7c:

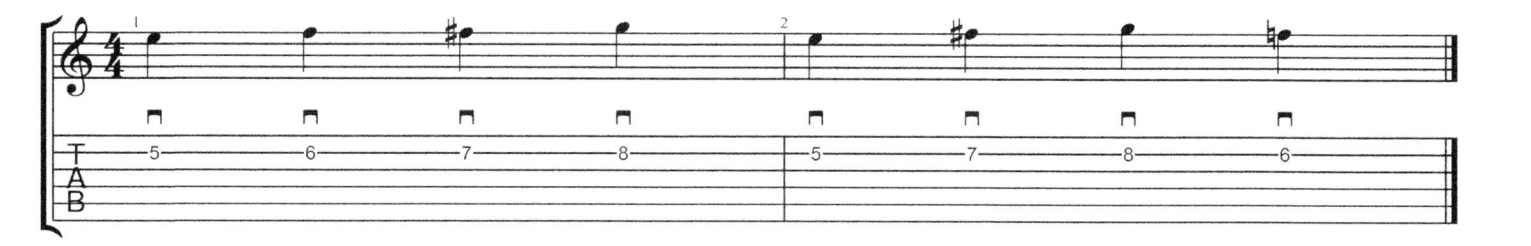

You used the minimum force required to play each note, eliminating the need for high pressure. The same relaxed state should also be applied to the thumb, mirroring this minimalist approach.

Continuing to retrain in this manner involves spending more time on simple exercises like the ones in this section, reminding yourself how little effort it takes to sound a note.

When you play exercises like this, the practice goal is to press down not one iota more than necessary. Choose a slow tempo like 80bpm and just keep repeating slow, graceful motions as you begin building better habits.

Example 7d:

The next goal is to be able to play at higher dynamic levels using pick strokes as the only variable method of attack. The picking hand needs to have zero influence over the pressure of the fretting hand.

Your fretting hand pressure should remain constant through Example 7e as the pick alternates between a moderate level of attack (bar one) and digging in a little harder for a stream of accented strokes (bar two).

If you feel yourself squeezing the fingers harder every time you pick accents, concentrate on separating that connection between the hands. Simple exercises like this will help you monitor fretting tension and release it as soon as you notice any.

Example 7e:

When you can break the co-dependency of fretting pressure and pick attack, the following separation exercise involves pressure and speed.

As the next drill alternates between 1/8th and 1/16th notes, the fretting hand should respond no differently.

Test this drill at multiple speeds, keeping those graceful fretting finger motions at all times.

Example 7f:

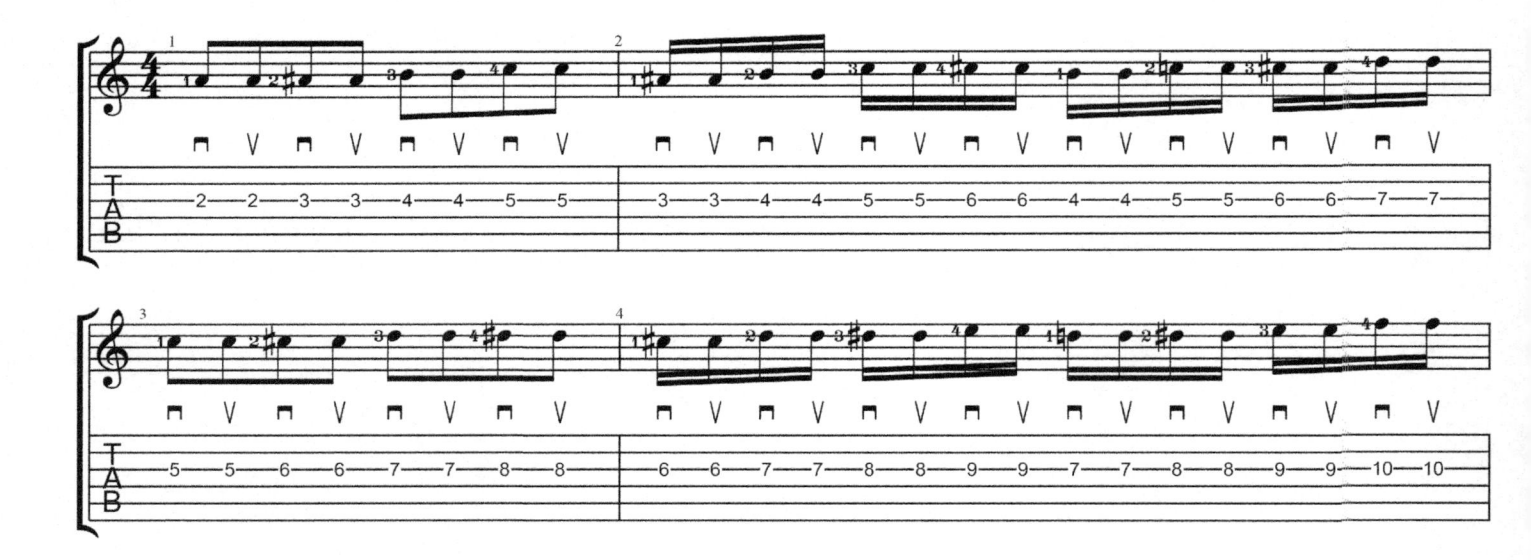

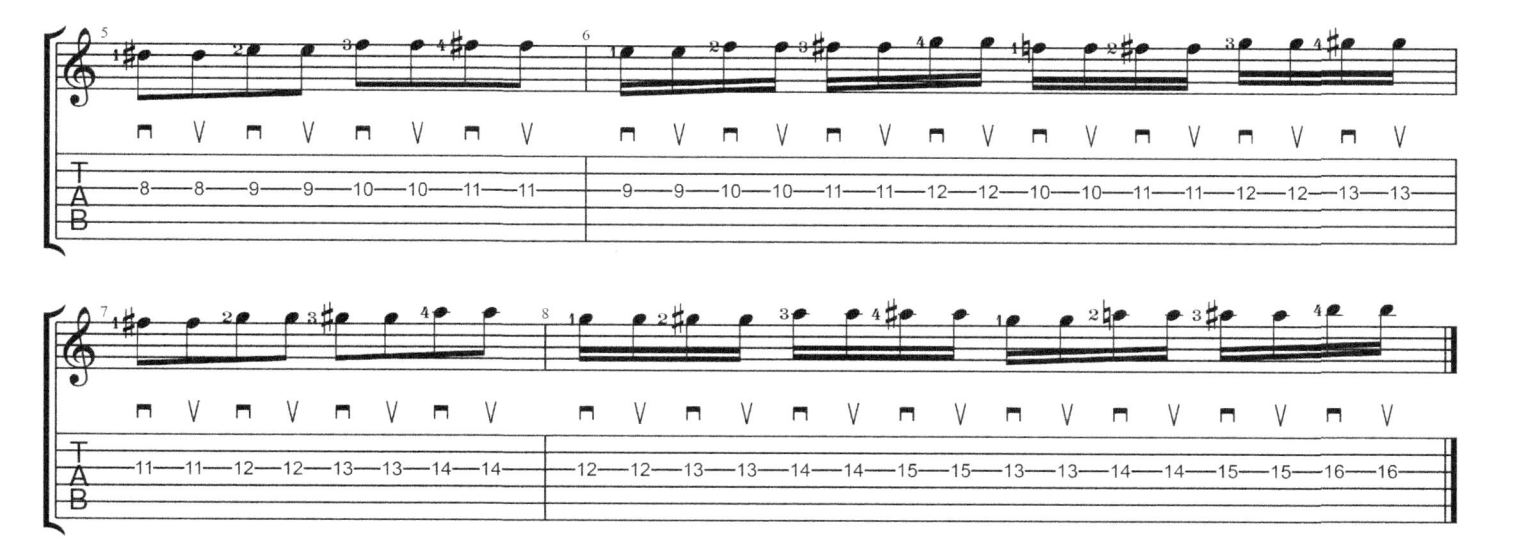

Using the retraining covered in this section, try to make relaxed (yet clear) fretting your default method to sound the notes in licks and scales.

Picking Hand Attack

Tension in the picking hand can emanate from multiple areas, so it's important to develop a good self-awareness of your muscles and recognise any problems, pre-existing or new.

Tension in your back, neck, shoulders, biceps and triceps, elbow, forearm, and wrist can be detrimental to guitar playing and vice versa. Have a good stretch and self-massage if you feel any issues before picking up a guitar. And, of course, seek treatment from a professional for persisting pain and tension.

What I'd love for you to get out of this section is what it feels like to pick without tension and use sustainable mechanics for everything you'd like to pick.

Let's start with gripping the pick to get you accustomed to picking without tension.

Pick grip should be firm but not tense. Grab your pick now, and let's try to find the optimum pressure.

Place your pick loosely between your thumb and index finger and gradually increase the pressure until your grip feels firm but not too stiff. If you see your inner or outer forearm flexing when you squeeze the pick, that's too much. Loosen up a little.

Using the thumb and finger of your other hand, try to wiggle the pick away from your picking hand. You may need to revise your pick grip if it slips out easily.

A grip that I find highly functional is one I refer to as the *curl grip* in my *Alternate Picking Guitar Technique* book.

The curl grip uses the side of the index finger, curled in to meet with the pad of the thumb. The surface area of the pick has a lot of contact with the finger and thumb, allowing a firm yet comfortable grip.

Figure 4:

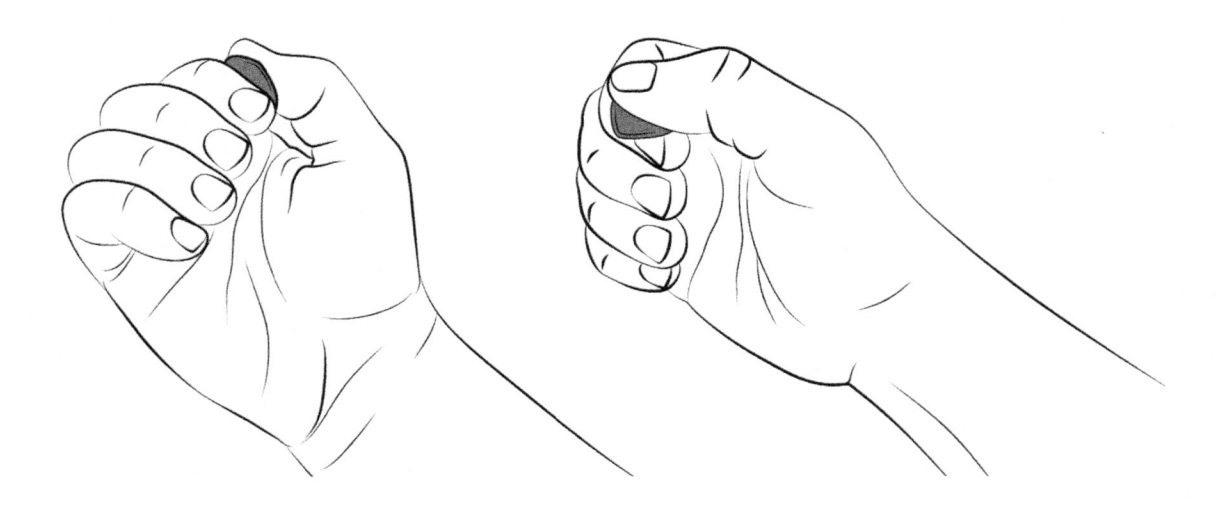

With the pick in place, the goal with dynamics is to be able to pick soft, hard, fast, or slow without affecting the pressure used to hold the pick.

Picking dynamics (i.e., the loudness or softness of pick strokes) aren't created by gripping the pick with different intensity levels but by how much of the pick is lowered into the string.

Just the tip of the pick creates the softest sound. Bringing it closer to the body of the guitar increases volume and attack.

As an exercise in dynamics, maintain a steady 1/8th note rhythm on a single note (Example 7g).

Begin with the smallest amount of contact between the pick and strings. With each beat, lower the tip of the pick a little further below the level of the strings, reaching a much higher volume by the end of bar three.

Repeat, immediately dropping back to a soft attack when bar one comes around each time. Control your timing, and don't let the changing contact between pick and strings slow you down or speed you up.

If any tension in your picking arm develops, ensure you're not squeezing the pick harder as the dynamic changes from soft to hard. Also, avoid pressing down harder with the fretting hand as the pick digs further into the strings.

It's okay to feel more of a particular muscle activating when the pick depth creates increased resistance, so long as it doesn't veer into tension, and especially not discomfort or pain. Feeling the difference is crucial to understanding how your body works and knowing when to stop and re-evaluate.

Watch the video to see a close-up of this example.

Example 7g:

A thin pick might start to flop around as you increase contact with the string, so consider a thicker pick if you're not getting a wide range of attack levels from your current one.

To compare hard and soft picking dynamics more directly, repeat examples 7h and 7i using only pick depth to create two different attack levels.

Example 7h:

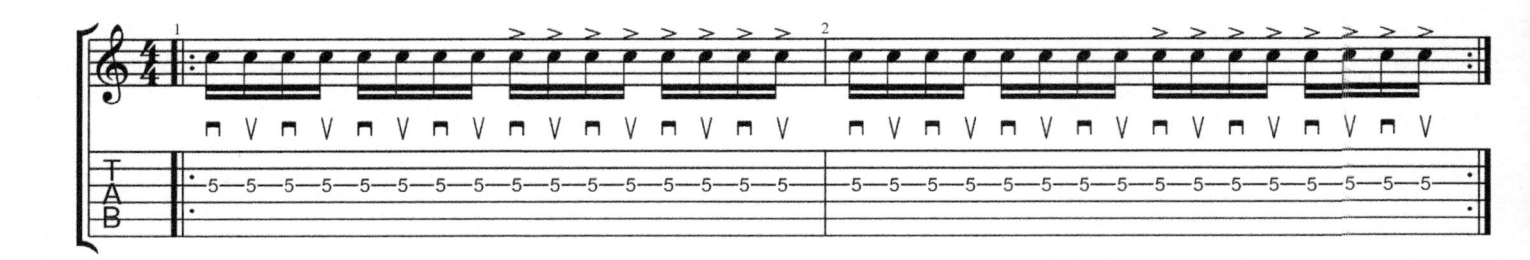

[Musical notation and tab: 4/4 time, two measures of sixteenth notes all on fret 5, with alternate picking (n V n V...) and accents (>) on the last 8 notes of each measure]

Example 7i:

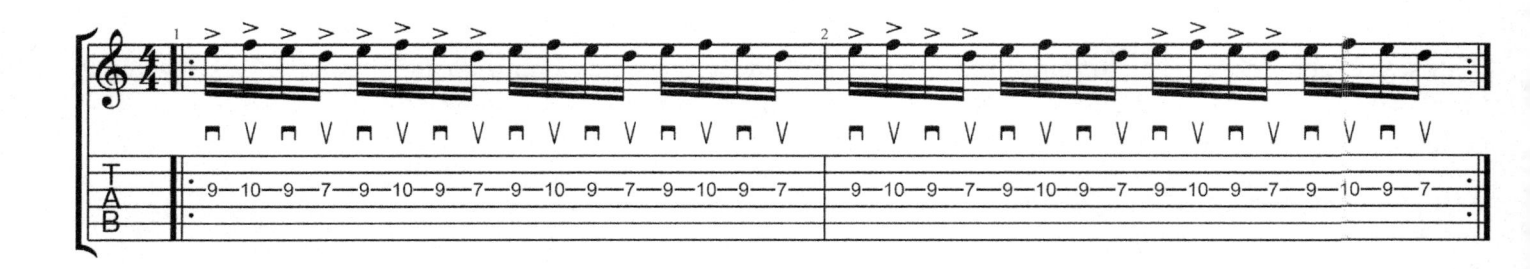

[Musical notation and tab: 4/4 time, two measures of sixteenth notes on frets 9-10-9-7 repeating, with alternate picking (n V n V...) and accents (>) pattern]

The final uncoupling to address in this chapter is tension and acceleration.

We've all seen speedy players and remarked on how relaxed they look. The relaxed factor isn't a coincidence but a significant contributor to being able to apply speed without cramping up straight away.

Whether someone's picking technique is based on the wrist, elbow, forearm motions or combinations thereof, speed increases don't need to be accompanied by increased tension.

If you've felt your muscles lock up or strain at higher speeds (or if you have trouble reaching high speed), try this tremolo picking experiment to monitor your picking technique as you accelerate and decelerate with this approach (Example 7j).

It won't matter what your minimum and maximum speeds are right now since the exercise is about the graduation of tempo while avoiding tension.

Tremolo picking a single note is an excellent way to put all your focus on the picking hand – what it's doing, how it feels, what changes occur etc. Controlled bursts of speed allow you to get exposure to the feel of playing fast while building good habits and improving endurance.

Try these steps.

1. Tremolo pick: one fret, one string (Example 7j), beginning at a steady, sustainable tempo

2. Maintain the same pick grip and pressure throughout

3. Accelerate by increasing the frequency of motions without gripping the pick tighter or straining the muscles

4. Bring the speed to the edge of your ability for a moment, then simmer down to the original speed and back up. Lighten the pick depth if you feel the pick resisting on the string too much

5. Monitor the feeling in your picking arm at all speeds, reminding yourself not to strain

6. End the process after a few rounds of speeding up and slowing down or when you feel any pain, whichever comes first

Example 7j:

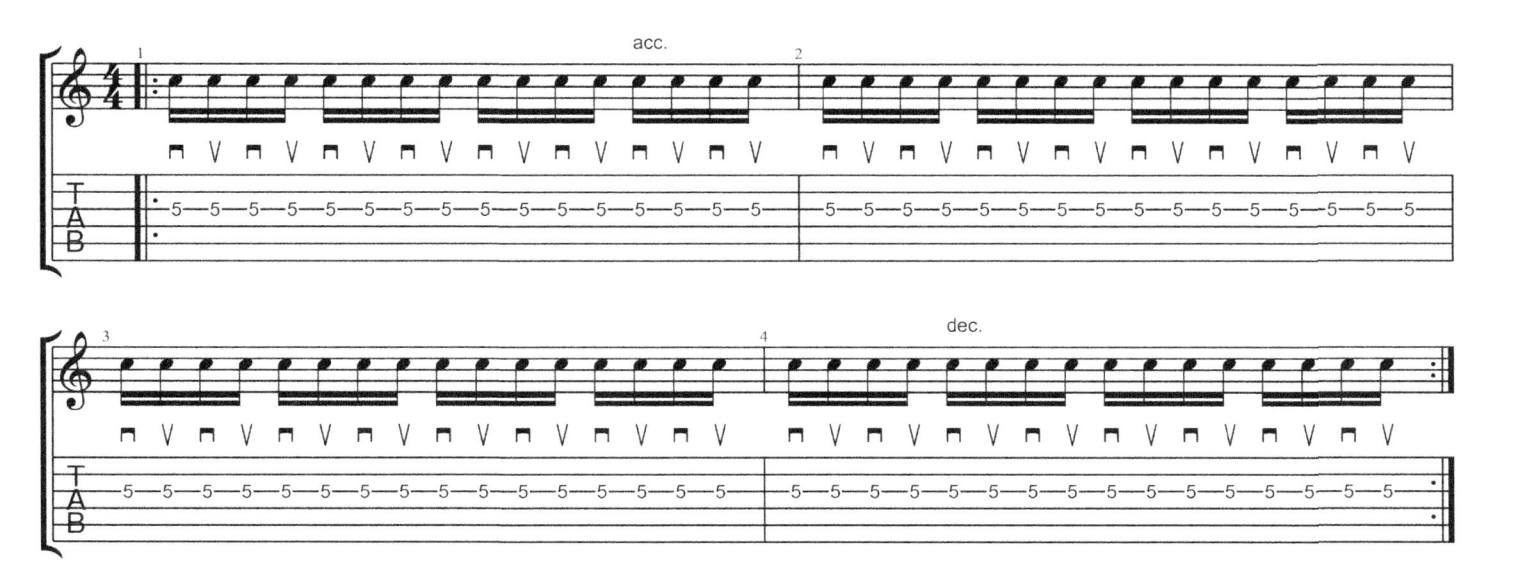

Example 7k:

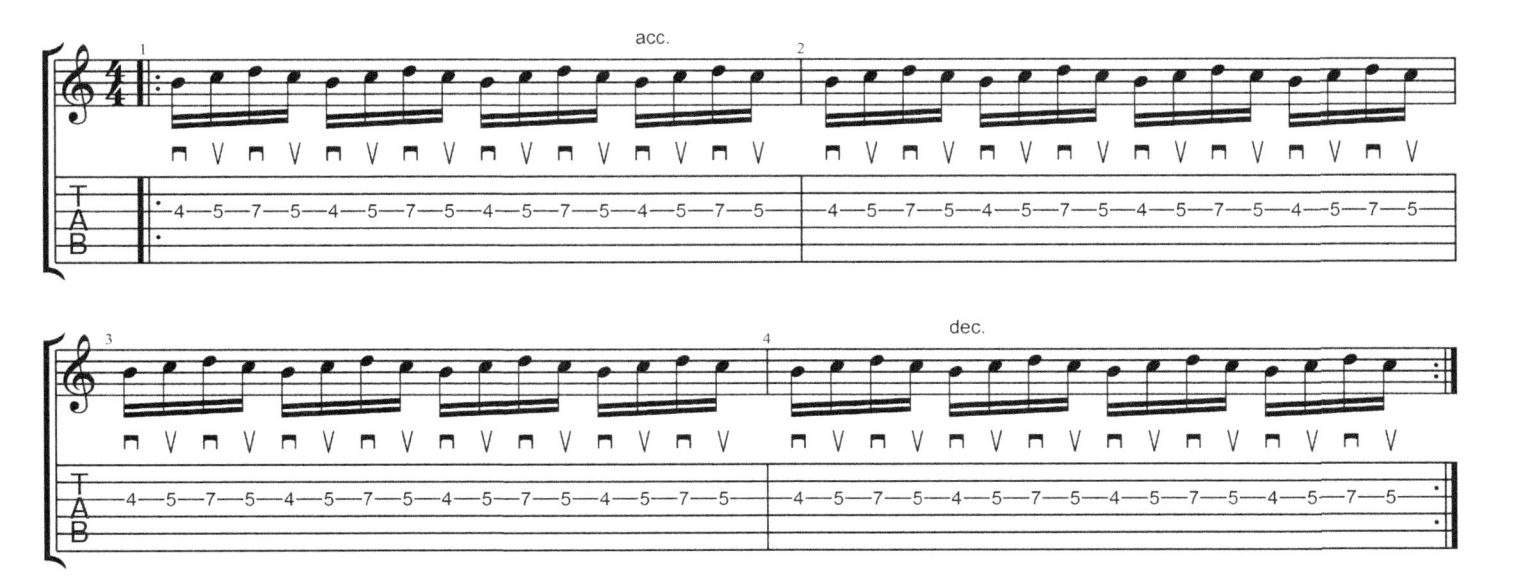

Repeat the process with separate notes for the fretting hand. If you're still feeling a lack of freedom in the picking hand at this point, check out the troubleshooting notes at the end of the chapter to reassess the functionality of your picking technique.

Across strings, accelerate and decelerate the repetition lick in Example 7l. Pick strokes are omitted because you can try this as an alternate- or economy-picked ostinato.

Example 7l:

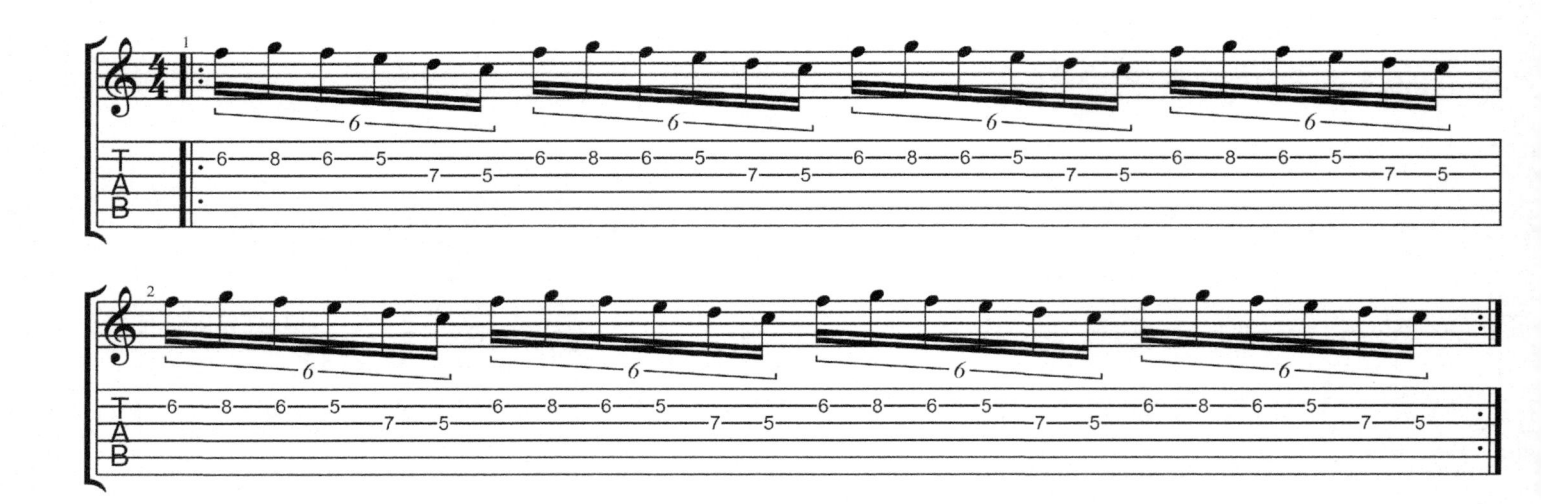

Throughout the chapters we've built good form, creating and improving synchronization and removing tension.

Good form is like programming, teaching your body commands and receiving feedback from it on the way things feel and sound. Those tools will be helpful as we delve into the strategies for creating speed in Chapter Eight.

Here are the most critical takeaways from this chapter:

- Tension is a hindrance to speed
- Ergonomic posture and positioning will give you the right start to comfortable playing
- The fretting hand only needs enough pressure to sound a clear note
- Picking hand dynamics are created with technique and resistance, not tension
- Fretting hand pressure should remain independent of picking dynamics
- Accents and speed can be applied without tensing up the muscles

Troubleshooting: Wayward Pick Strokes

There isn't just one way to pick fast from a mechanical perspective, as you'll notice from comparing the wrist picking of Al Di Meola and John McLaughlin, the elbow picking of Vinnie Moore and Rusty Cooley, and the wrist-forearm-finger blend of Yngwie Malmsteen.

What the best speedsters do have in common is a command of logical pick motion that avoids scooping in and out of the strings on every stroke.

Observe your baseline picking motion now by either tremolo-picking one note or playing any of the single-string drills you've worked on.

If the pick moves in and out of the strings in a U-shape, like Figure 5, you're working too hard and it's costing you time and speed.

Figure 5:

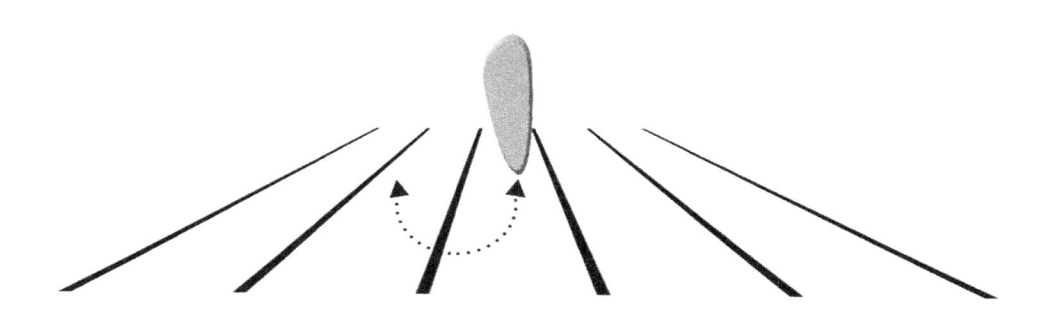

Straight-line picking is the most economical (and, therefore, fastest) way to pick up and down on a string.

Sometimes we need to angle the straight line picking motion to get the pick out of the strings after an upstroke, and other times after a downstroke, according to where the lick goes next. Along one-string, U-shaped picking is unnecessary.

Here is an illustration of angled, straight-line picking on the G string, moving below the surface of the strings on downstrokes and above it on upstrokes.

Players like Eric Johnson, Mike Stern, Yngwie Malmsteen and yours truly pick along this pathway a great deal of the time and structure a lot of picking lines to remain in this orientation.

Figure 6:

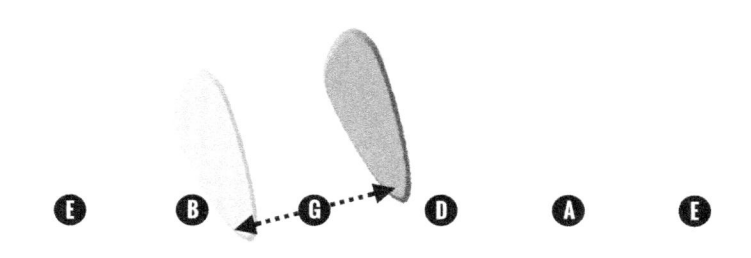

And here is the pick moving *above the surface of the strings* on downstrokes and below it on upstrokes. You'll see this trajectory used in the picking lines of Al Di Meola, Vinnie Moore, Andy James, and Rusty Cooley. It's just as effective as the previously illustrated direction.

Figure 7:

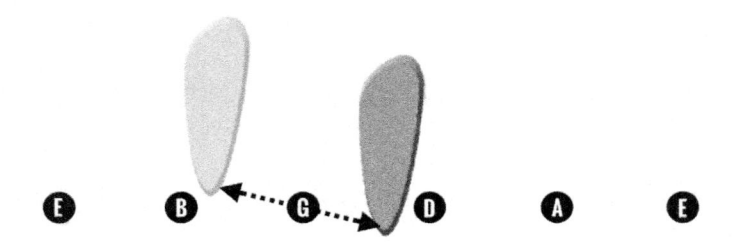

Both trajectories are demonstrated in the bonus video.

To adopt a straighter line of motion in your picking, revisit examples 7j and 7k. Monitor where each downstroke finishes, then double back along the same pathway for the upstroke.

If you notice a U-shape creeping back into the picking motion, stop, begin again, and speed up. You'll know if it's working because your tremolo picking will feel easier, more logical, and less of a strain.

Alternate Picking Guitar Technique (and my optional video expansion pack) contains modules on picking lines that change strings after upstrokes, downstrokes, and mixed strokes to help you overcome the challenges of each.

Chapter Eight: The Speed Practice System

This is where your chops and timing will be tested and pushed to advance your top speed and increase the comfort you feel at your current limits. With this system, you should see results even within a single session.

I'll give you the drills I used in my development and tell you exactly how to try them. These exercises don't equate to high art in terms of musical expression but, as mentioned in the intro to this section, speed is a subject to pursue separately. The music is where you use it as you choose.

After breaking the system down, I'll explain how to apply it to other things you might be playing.

The best way to understand the practice system is to compare steady-state cardio with high-intensity interval training (HIIT).

Steady-state cardio workouts involve performing an exercise for a prolonged period at a sustainable intensity for the whole session. HIIT workouts are shorter, where bursts of intense exercise are done with intermittent breaks – pushing the body hard in small intervals with alternating rest periods.

The body can't sustain HIIT levels for the same duration as steady-state cardio, but some studies consider HIIT up to nine times more effective for fat burning.

The system here won't have you seeing how many burpees you can do in sixty seconds before giving you a thirty-second break. It will, however, involve exceeding your current limit in bursts and providing your nerves with some quick intervals to reset.

My process is based on the concept of modified practice – the idea that you get better at a skill not by repeating it the same way endlessly but by coming up with modifications that make the original idea more embedded in your muscle memory.

Some things to keep in mind before proceeding:

- You need to learn the drills ahead before you speed them up. You can't master what you don't know. The good news is that they're all conceptually simple

- Speed is relative to your own goals and ability. I won't be telling you that tempo X is slow and tempo Y is better. This system works on percentages so that you can use it at any level

- Self-awareness is your best friend in this material. Be honest with yourself about how things are sounding

- It's going to get a bit messy. To push chops into new territory, they need to be challenged. There's an acceptable level of error permitted with this system, which I'll detail soon

- Never play through injury. Just don't. You can't out-practice pain. Seek treatment or even try a timeout if you develop issues

Zip files for your mind

The examples presented for speed development are comprised of short, repeated units, four or six notes in many cases.

When you've learnt a phrase, your brain will process information faster and more efficiently when groups of notes are remembered as one piece of information to process. Think of it as zip files for your mind – compact and singular for moving around.

So, when a bar of sixteen notes contains the same four-note phrase repeated four times, think in terms of four blocks or chunks rather than sixteen individual pieces of information. Focus on timing each block in the precise spot each time and use the rest of your brain to consider things like tone, attack, timing etc.

In cognitive psychology and neuroscience, the process of compacting information in this way is called *chunking*. Thinking in larger pieces allows faster processing, just as the folders of a zip file are optimised for ease of online delivery.

You've probably been doing this without knowing it for many examples in the book. The exercises have become less about remembering individual notes and more about controlling how all the pieces come together.

When you've learnt the individual components of a lick, joined them in blocks, then practiced connecting the blocks, you'll feel a sense of autonomy when playing the licks. People refer to it as "muscle memory", but this is your brain functioning more economically too.

Now that you know how to think faster, here are the steps we'll proceed with to *play* more quickly.

The Speed Practice System includes five stages (and an optional sixth):

1. Determine your current top speed of a steady-state repetition lick
2. Turn the lick into an interval lick with breaks
3. Accelerate the interval lick by a given percentage for burst practice
4. Increase the tempo (stage 4.1), then again (stage 4.2), and possibly once more (stage 4.3)
5. Return to the tempo used in stage 3 and try to establish it as your new top speed
6. Apply exaggeration modifications to stages 1-5, where possible

Finding your continuous top speed

For the sake of the system, your current continuous top speed is the tempo at which you can perform at least four bars of exact repeats without falling out of sync or getting sloppy. Don't overestimate or underestimate this number because it's important for the process to work.

To find your continuous top speed (let's call it CTS from now on), repeat the drill from a comfortable pace, accelerating to your limit throughout a few bars. Don't do metronome work yet because you don't want repetition fatigue this early on.

When you think you've found the limit – the highest point at which you're holding it together and not getting sloppy and unsynchronized – figure out what that tempo is on your metronome.

To confirm your CTS, play continuously at the tempo you've set for ten seconds or so. If it feels like you're holding back, set the metronome a little faster. Bring the tempo down if it feels like you're starting to fake it to keep up with the click. That's your confirmed CTS.

Let's follow the process with the examples ahead.

The first series of drills use alternate picking because of its popularity as a foundational guitar technique. Later, I'll refer back to other techniques and how you can apply this approach.

Application: Single Strings

The first drill is a 1-2-3-4 chromatic scale fragment using each finger. The aim is to increase the single-string speed of the picking hand while maintaining one note per pick stroke with the fretting hand.

After an adequate warm-up (Section One has plenty of material for that), it's time to determine your CTS using the earlier steps. Use the four fingers of the fretting hand to play the 7th, 8th, 9th, and 10th frets on the B string in repetition.

Find the tempo you topped at on the metronome, then double-check your CTS by playing Example 8a to the click. A rest is included at the end of bar two to ensure fatigue is not slowing you down.

If you're not playing with an overall accuracy of ninety to ninety-five per cent, you may have overestimated your CTS. Lower the metronome a couple of clicks and try again.

Example 8a:

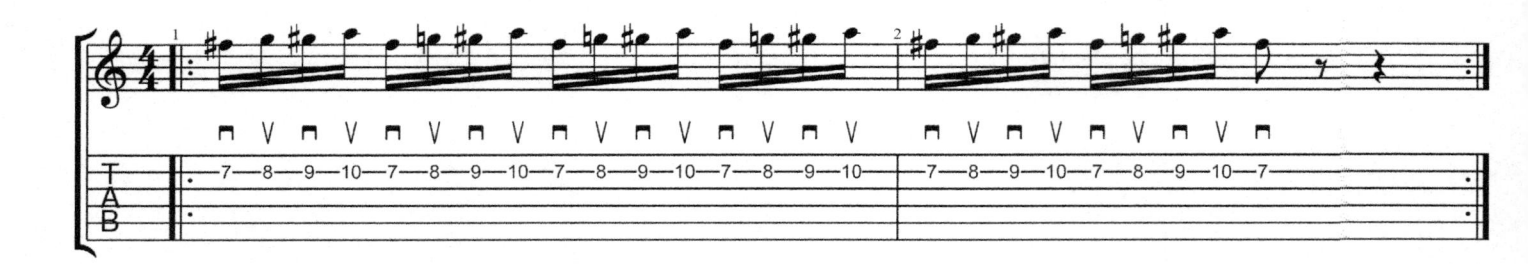

Now that you have a starting tempo, work through the steps of the system.

For stage two, modify the drill to alternate between picking and rests. You can begin with longer rests like bars one, two, and four, or increase the frequency of the phrase like bar three.

Accents have been added to emphasise the importance of locking your "chunks" into the beat.

Example 8b:

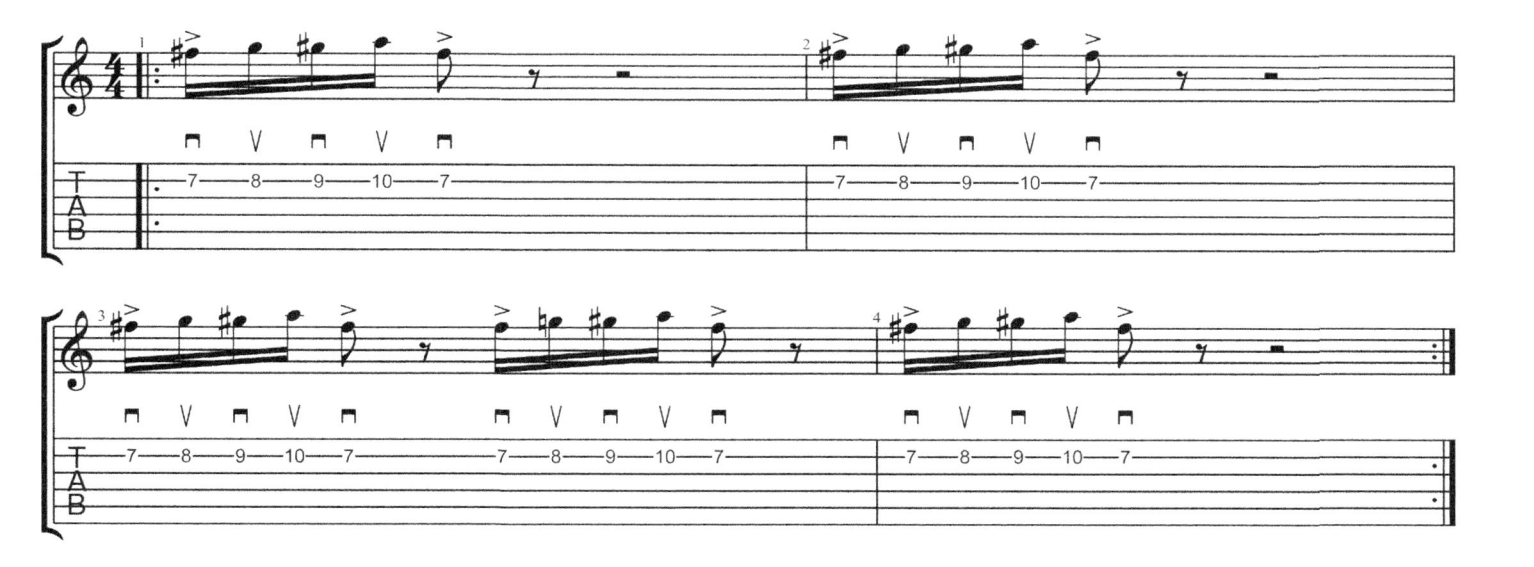

For stages three and four, increase the original CTS by a compound percentage of ten per cent each time. Multiply each tempo by 1.1 to get the next number.

If your CTS in Example 8a was 125bpm, stage three means Example 8b would be 138bpm.

Play Example 8b at the new tempo eight times in succession (i.e., thirty-two bars), using the rests to take the pressure out of your hands. Launch into each bar at the precise time. Don't come in early for the sake of cheating the metronome.

For stage four, add another ten per cent to the cumulative tempo each time. For our example CTS of 125bpm and stage three tempo of 138bpm, the metronome will go up to 151bpm, followed by 166bpm.

If you're not performing stage four at a minimum success rate of about eighty per cent, use the short rests to tell yourself what to focus harder on. For example, "Make sure the third finger lands on that third 1/16th note."

The more correct repeats you perform, the better the habits you build. There's a fine line between learning to correct errors at speed and just reinforcing mistakes through repetition. Be diligent, and your body will try to find a way to solve issues as long as you don't turn a blind eye.

If you can get one more tempo increase (stage 4.3) out of this process, you may have underestimated your original CTS or not been thoroughly warmed up at the beginning. Or you may just be awesome, bursting at forty-six per cent above your original CTS in one practice session!

To see if you've gained speed through today's work, test Example 8a at the tempo you first used for Example 8b. This is the fifth stage of the process.

If you have made gains, congratulations! Imagine what will be possible when you make this a regular part of your workouts. If not, spend more time on one of the higher bursting tempos and recheck it.

When you do the routine again tomorrow, determine your CTS from scratch and follow the steps again. In string-changing examples, I'll add a sixth stage to the routine.

Here are some sample increments to make it easier to run through this process without a calculator.

CTS (bpm)	Stage 3 Bursts	Stage 4.1	Stage 4.2	Stage 4.3	New CTS
80	88	97	106	117	88
95	104	115	126	139	104
110	121	133	146	161	121
125	138	151	166	183	138
140	154	169	186	205	154
160	176	194	213	234	176

Now that you understand the process, let's continue with more drills.

Example 8c is an ascending and descending position-shifting exercise. You'll not only have to synchronize the fretting but also the slides.

Example 8c:

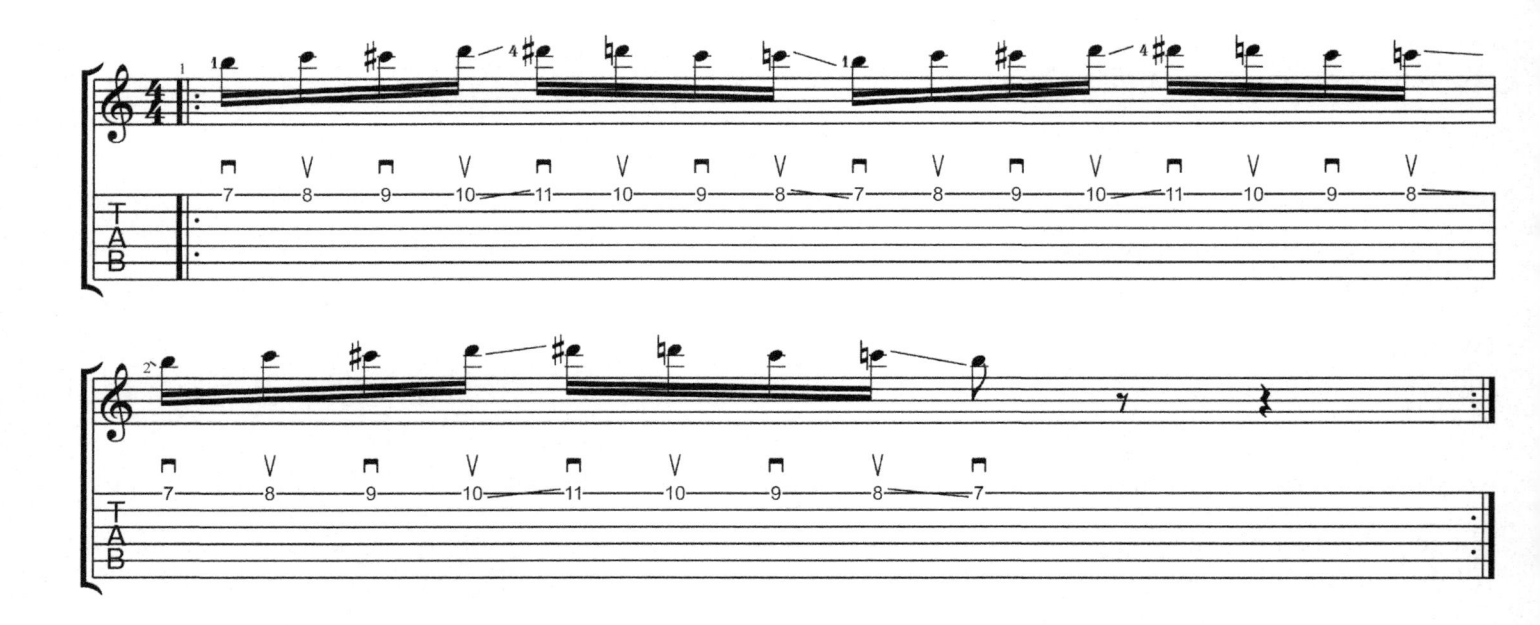

For the burst version, use this variation. Bars one and two isolate the ascending and descending portions, while bars three and four combine them in intervals.

Don't be concerned if your CTS is lower than the previous example since the degree of difficulty is higher. Each lick needs to be treated as a project unto itself with the overall goal of increased general speed.

Example 8d:

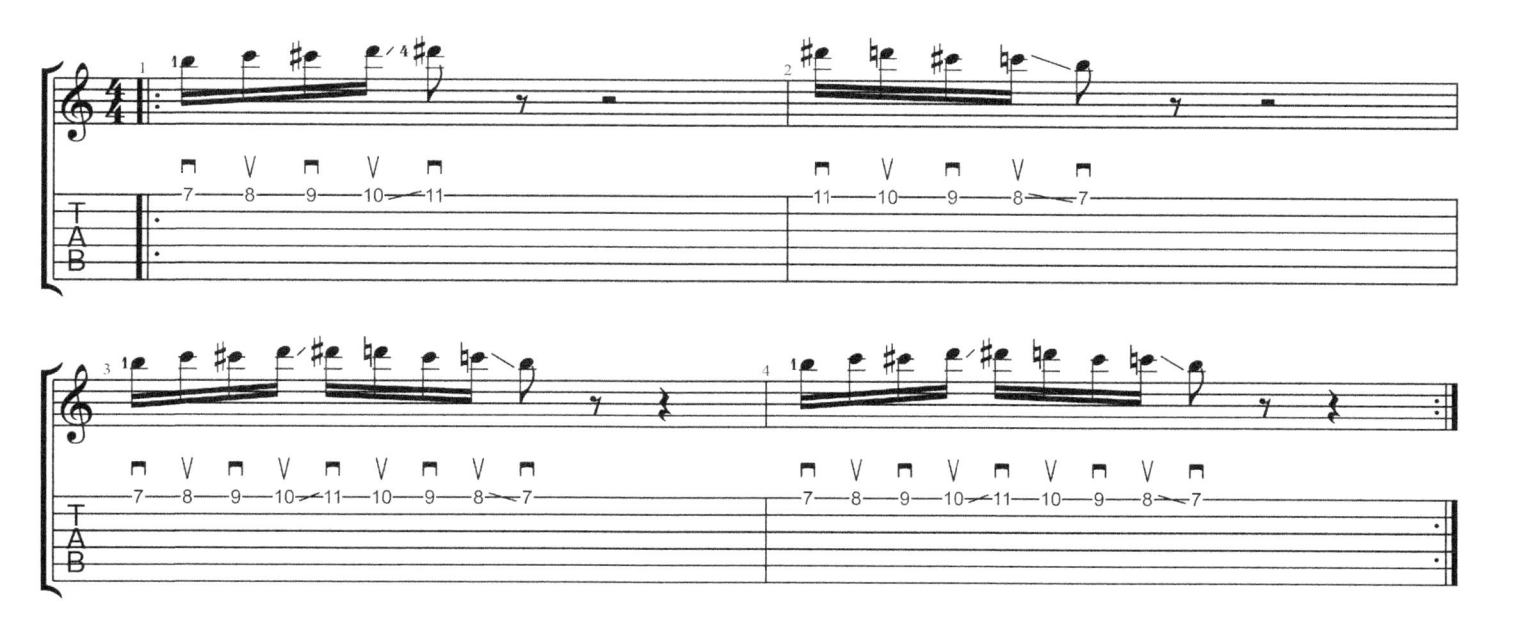

For groups of six on single strings, here's a three-note fingering that moves diatonically up and down the G string.

Example 8e:

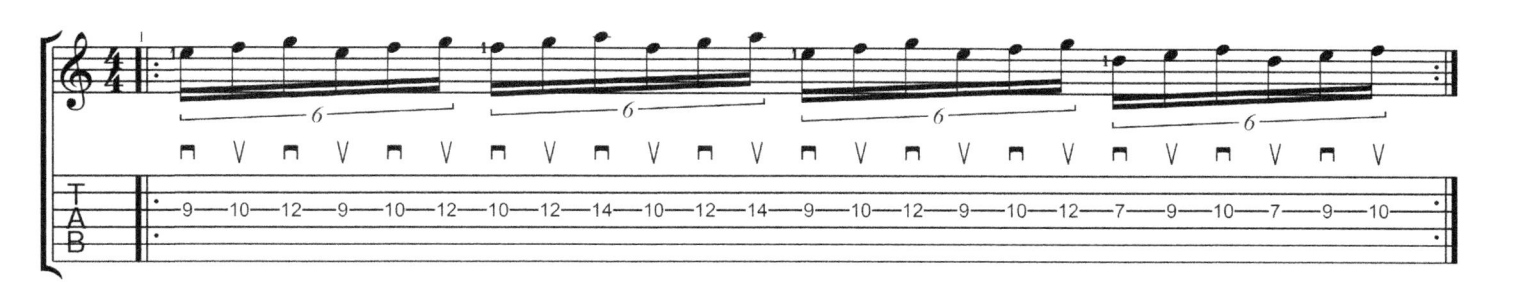

With bursts and rests, we can try a version like this.

Example 8f:

Examples 8g and 8h provide the descending versions of the two previous examples.

Example 8g:

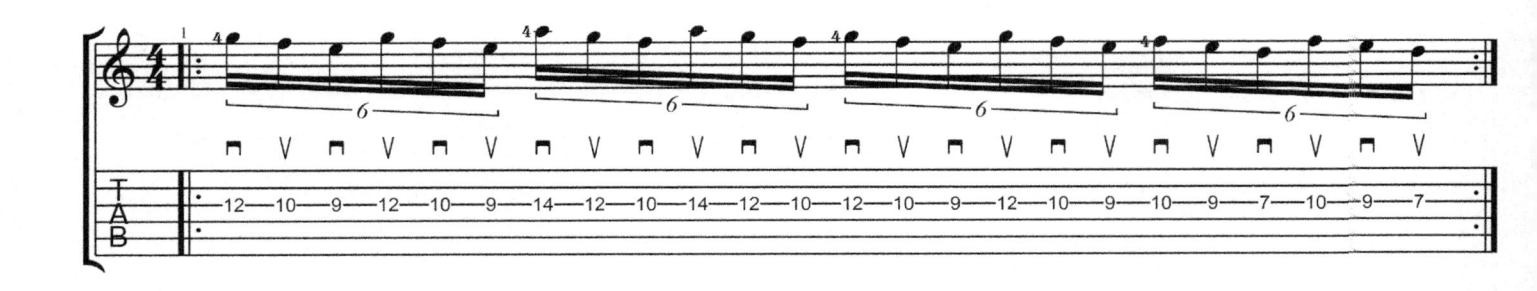

Example 8h:

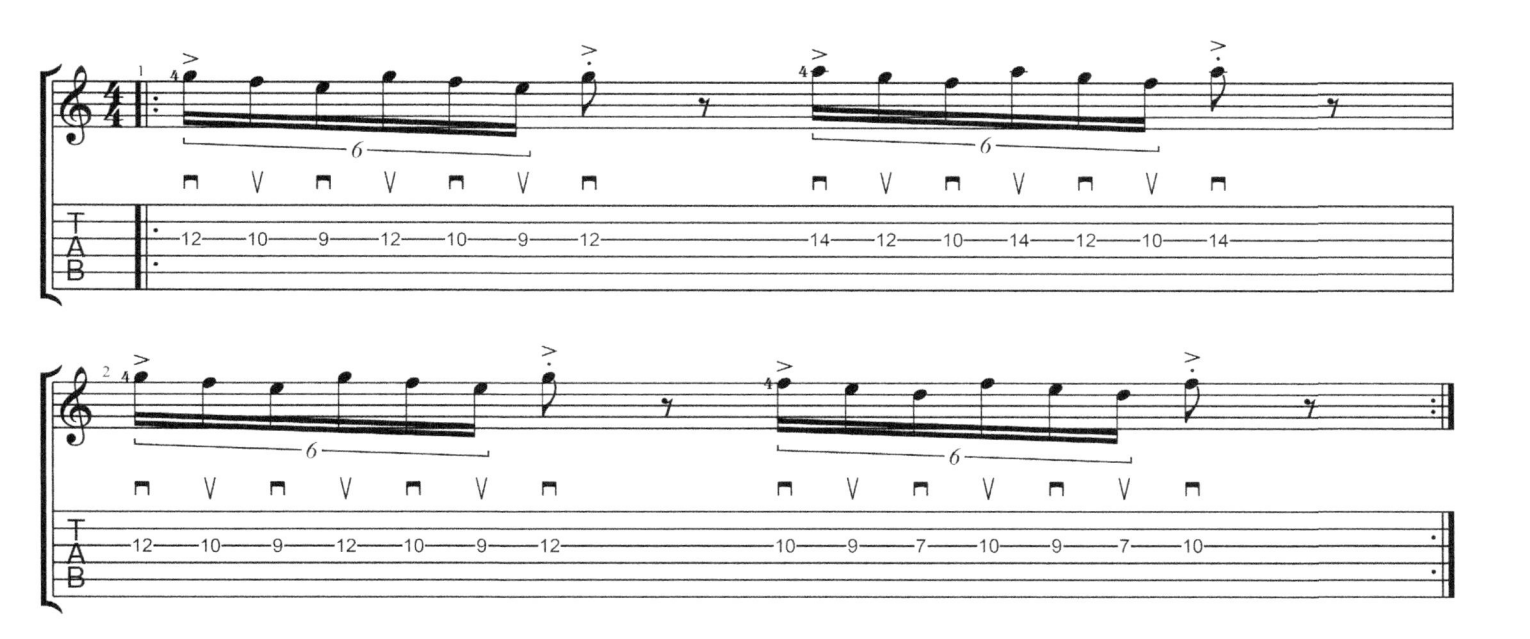

To get some melodic mileage out of the position-shifting drills in Example 8c, here's an A Harmonic Minor sequence on the high E string (Example 8i) followed by its interval-training variation (Example 8j).

Example 8i:

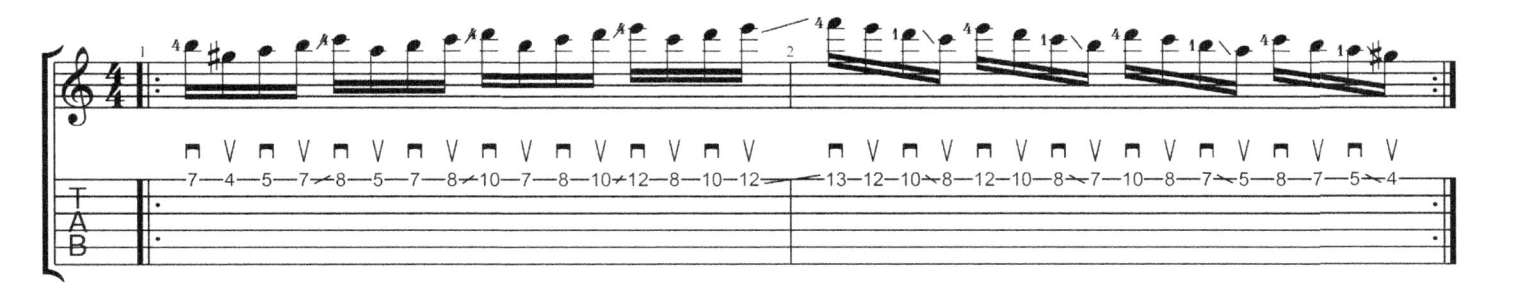

Example 8j:

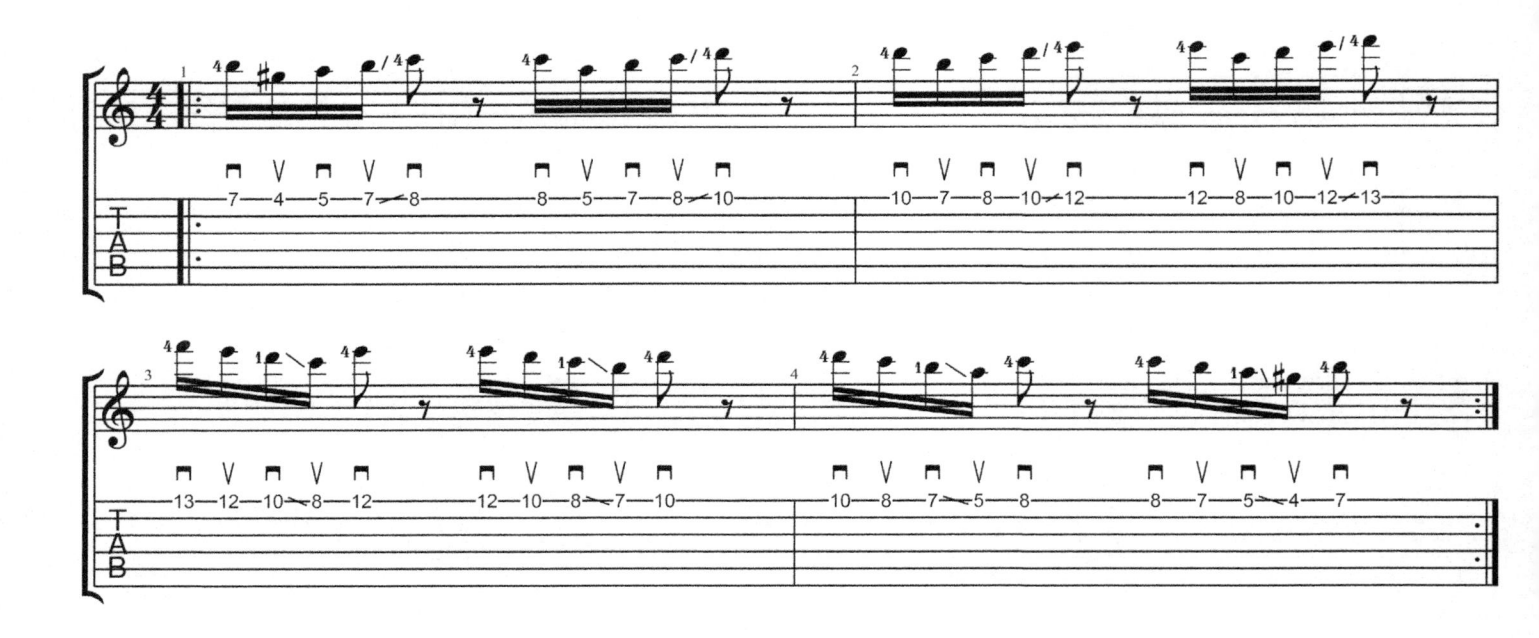

If you need more rest time in your intervals, you can modify burst examples as follows.

Example 8k:

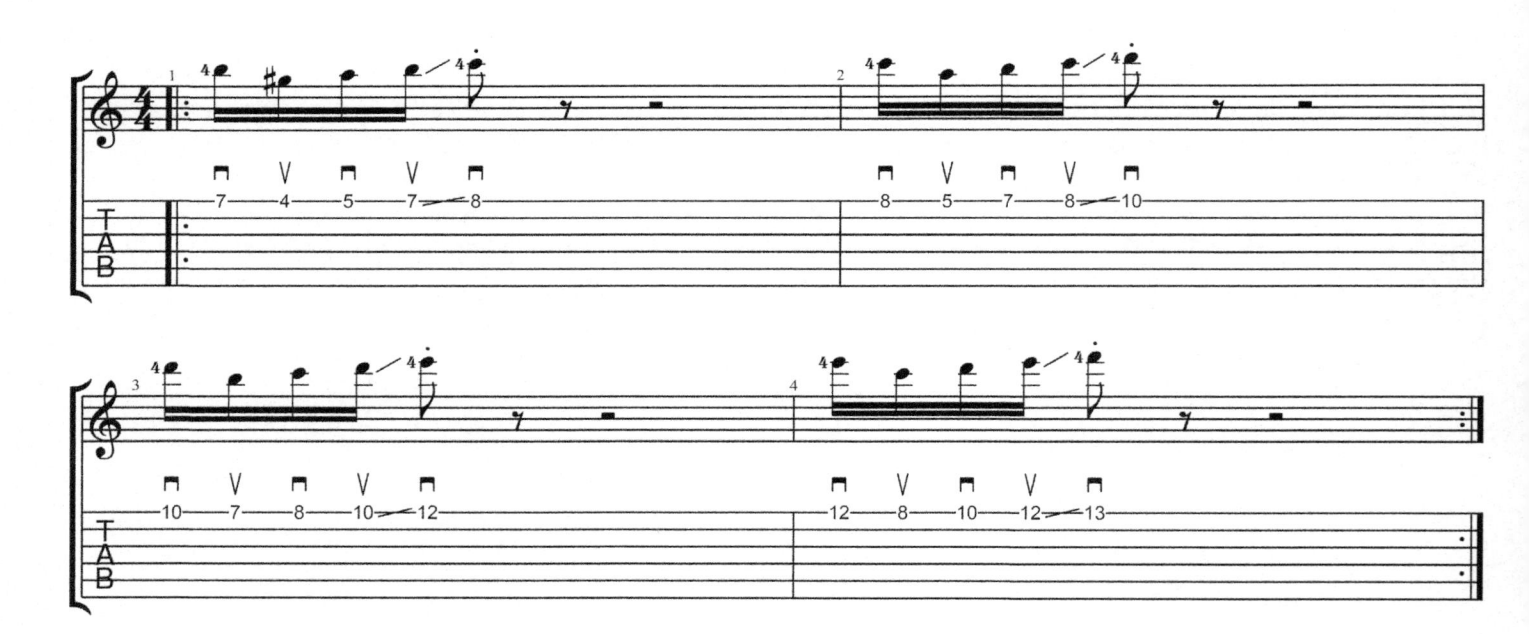

The chicken and egg of "small movements"

It's sometimes theorised that to pick fast, you need to start with a small motion. I would disagree and suggest that while a small motion is a great visual indicator that a player has sharpened their process to a point where motion is less visible, refinement is a product of the speed they've acquired – not the other way around.

When newer players become overly concerned with how their motion looks instead of exploring its potential speed, it creates a prolonged period where the player feels like everything *should* be working without knowing if it is. Instead, you'll achieve speed by testing for speed.

In most situations, the technique that works is the right one. If your pick strokes are flying out as 1/16th notes at 220bpm, your picking has no choice but to cut the fat of excess motion. Trust the process and get fast first, then see what additional improvements you can make.

Application: String Changes

String-changing licks can not only benefit from the first five stages of the speed practice system but from an extra exaggeration stage.

Here's a Paul-Gilbert style drill on the D and G strings using outside picking for the string change.

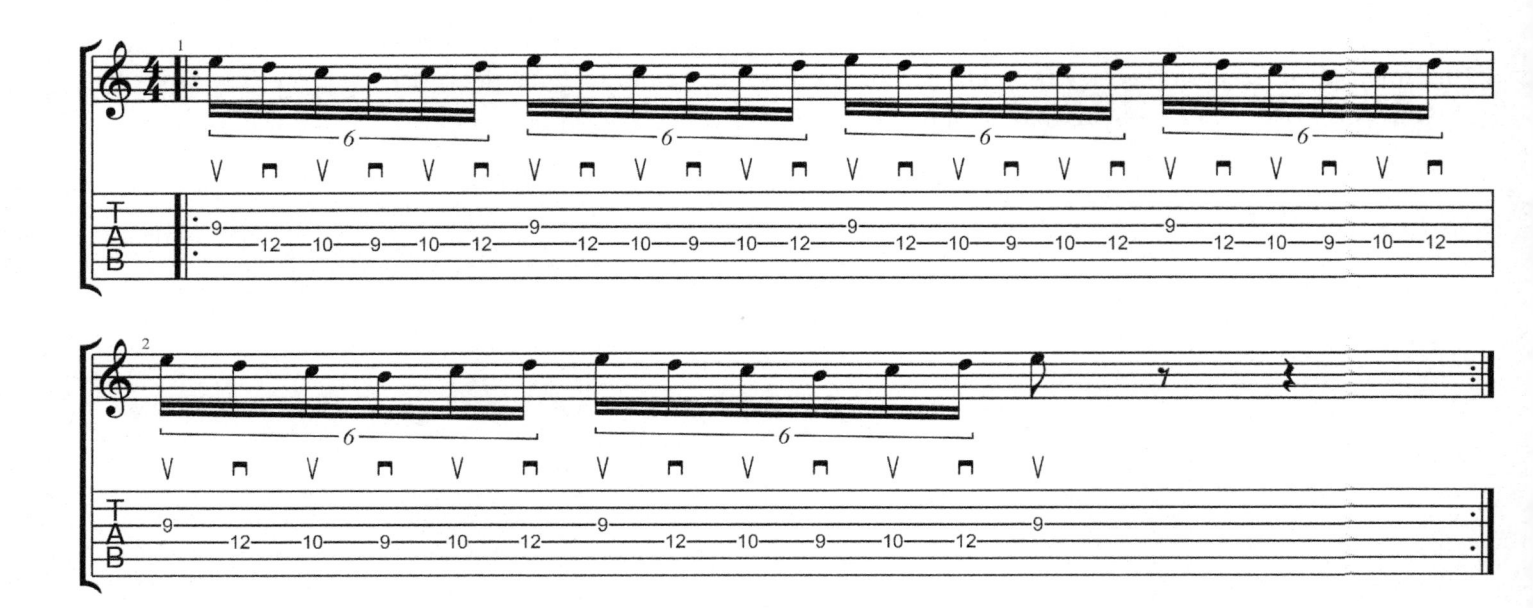

Example 8l:

Determine your CTS for the above lick, then try this variation for the burst stages.

Example 8m:

After completing stage five of the practice system, the previous drill can be exaggerated with string-skipping as a sixth stage with bursts and tempo increases. Don't be concerned if Example 8n is much harder and slower than Example 8m since the string distance is now doubled.

Also, don't worry about adjacent string noise too much. The aim is to make those string changes on time, then use the exaggeration to make Example 8l easier and faster.

Example 8n:

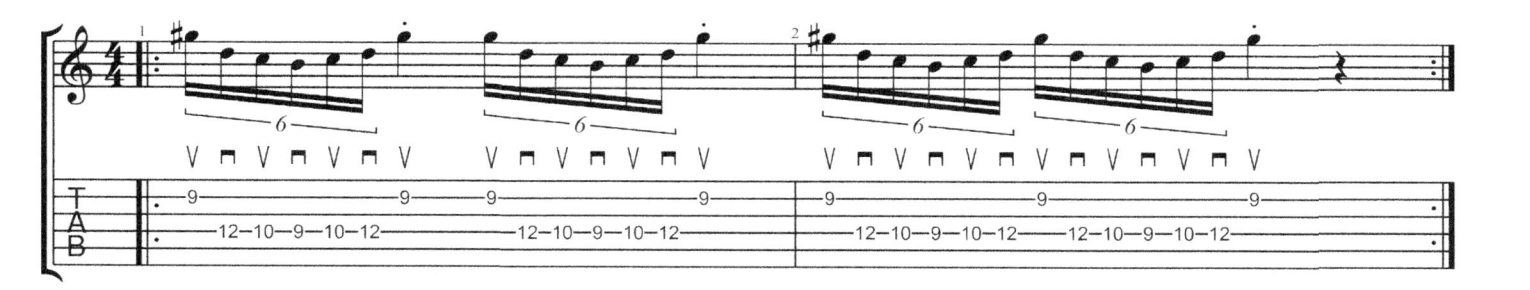

```
       9-------------9-------------9-------------9-------------9-------------9-------------9-------------9-------
    12-10-9-10-12-------12-10-9-10-12-------12-10-9-10-12-------12-10-9-10-12-
```

V ⊓ V ⊓ V   V ⊓ V ⊓ V   V ⊓ V ⊓ V ⊓ V ⊓ V ⊓ V

Moving on, here's a sextuplet lick in two octaves, beginning with a downstroke for each six.

Example 8o:

```
                                                      10—12—14——  10—12—14——
                                          10—12—14——  10—12—14——
                          8—10—12——  8—10—12——
    8—10—12——  8—10—12——
```

⊓ V ⊓ V ⊓ V ⊓ V ⊓ V ⊓ V ⊓ V ⊓ V ⊓ V ⊓ V ⊓ V ⊓ V

To incorporate exaggerating into the burst stages right from the get-go, try this version through the steps of the practice routine.

You'll be brushing past numerous strings to make the more significant jumps but just focus on making the string changes happen.

Example 8p:

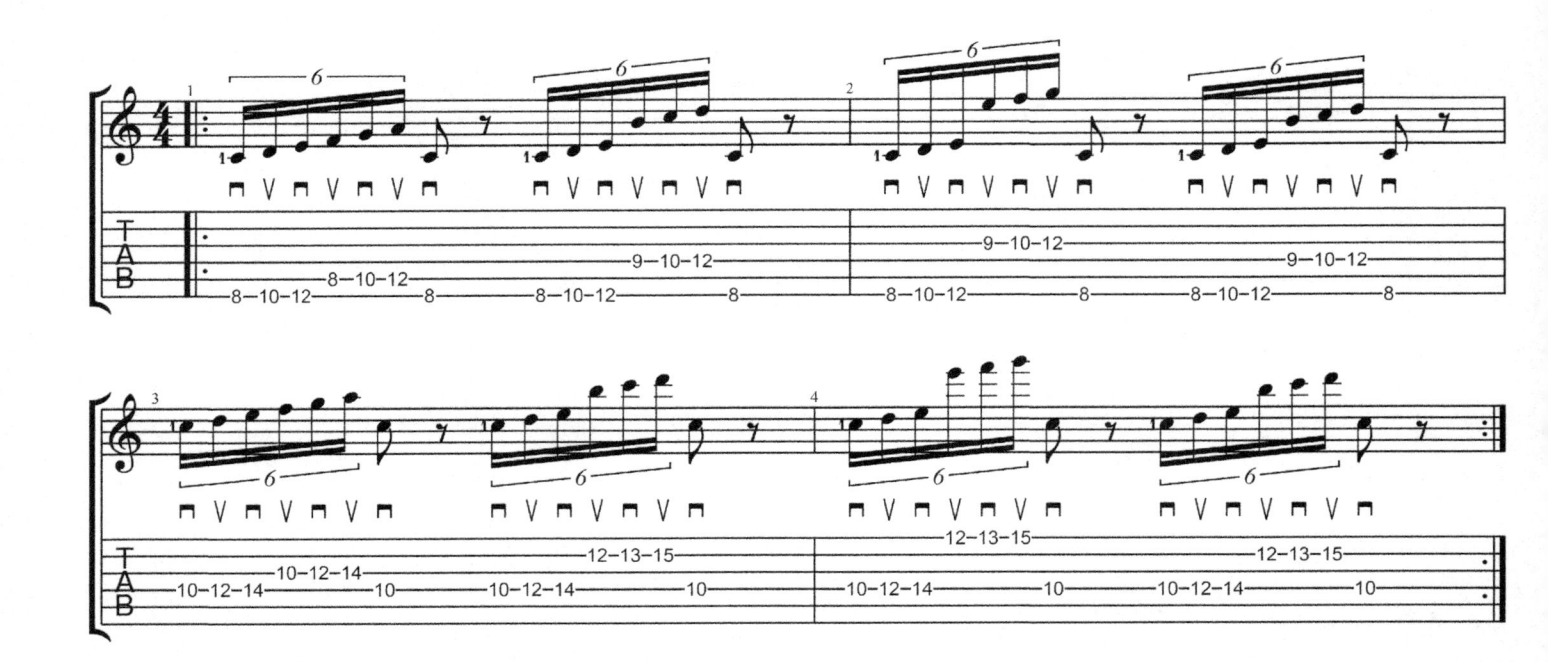

To turn examples 8l to 8p into inside picking drills, reverse the pick strokes and work them through the routine. You can also use them as legato and picking exercises by picking only the first note of each string.

Let's turn our attention to economy picking for Examples 8q and 8r. Here's a steady state drill with all-sweeping string changes.

Example 8q:

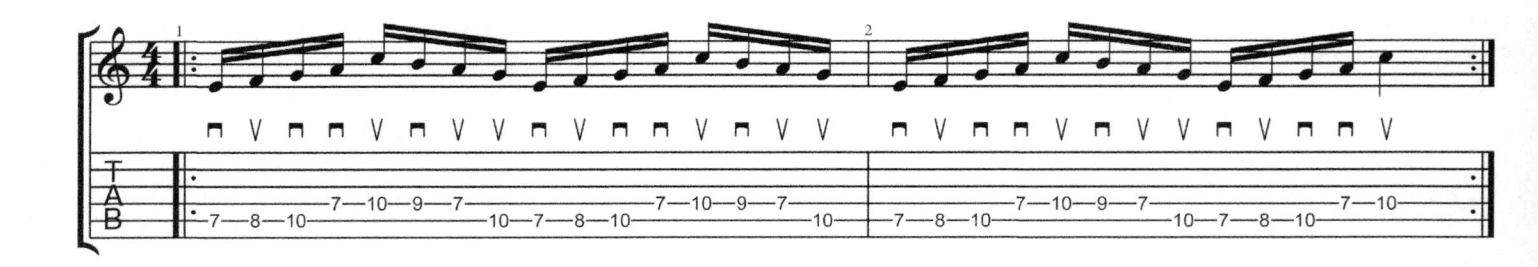

And, of course, that will give us an interval training burst of:

Example 8r:

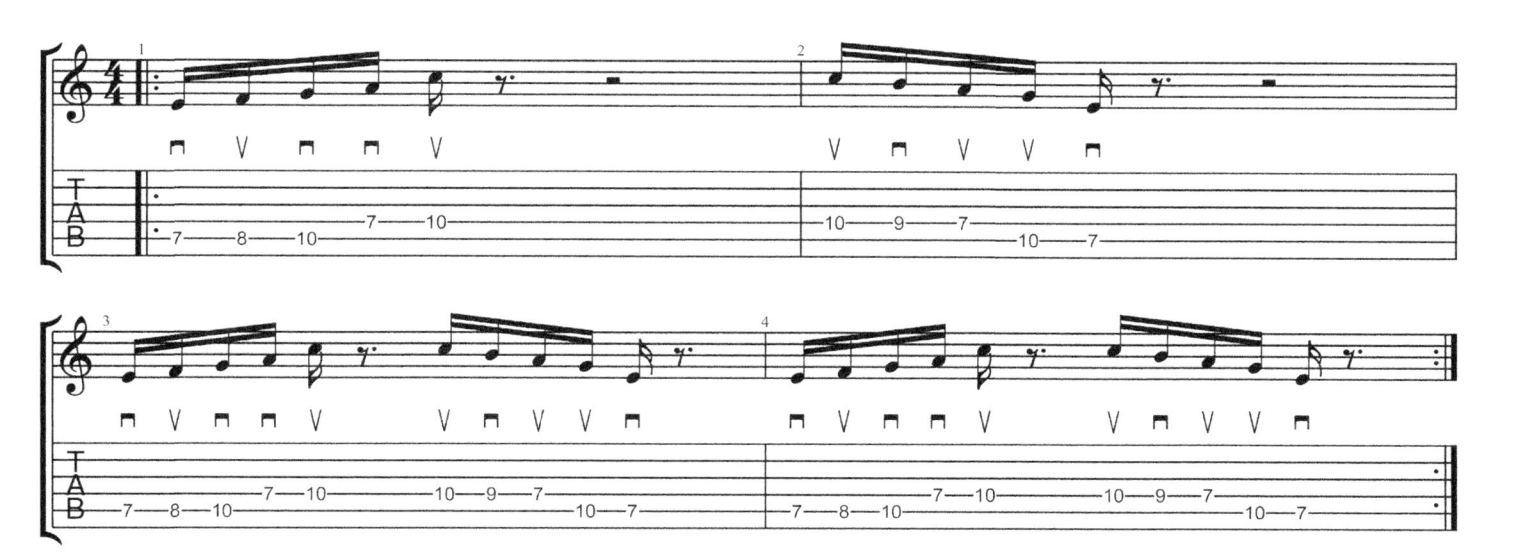

To construct a speed-building practice routine as I've described, do the following:

- Warm up properly using material from Section One or other stuff you're working on

- Choose three drills from this chapter

- Determine the CTS of your first choice

- Work it through the acceleration and burst stages of the process, spending as much (but not more) time as you need on each tempo. Eight good repeats will indicate whether you're ready to move on or need to do more work

- Repeat the routine for the two other drills you've chosen

- Make a note of your new CTS for each lick at the end of the session

- Choose new drills the next day or continue to see how fast you can get today's material in your next session

- See what other licks you can run through this system, whether they be other different techniques, your own licks, or segments of solos you're working on

Other Speed Practice Strategies

My Speed Practice System isn't the only way to get exposure to more speed and push yourself in measured bursts.

"Double-speed bursts" and "subdivision bursts" are two other strategies I've had success with as a player and teacher. These work particularly well for keeping your chops in good condition when practice time is an issue.

Double-speed bursts combine slow and steady work for synchronization and blasts for challenging speed.

The idea is to play something with a particular subdivision and focus on perfecting the sound and timing of the drill, then halve the subdivisions for a stretch, giving the impression that the tempo doubled.

This approach provides a great contrast between what you're doing at slow and fast speeds.

Example 8s is a three-string alternate picking pattern that switches from 1/8th notes to 1/16th notes. Choose a tempo that challenges you. For example, if your CTS for bar three is 180bpm, play the whole lick at, or above, 190bpm so that the 1/16th note bursts give you exposure to reaching a new level.

For extra work, make it a legato or economy picking drill too.

Example 8s:

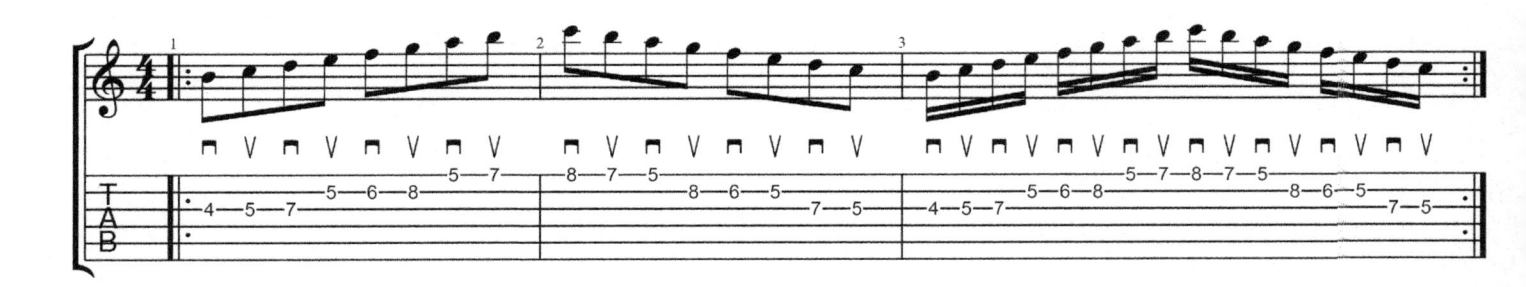

Example 8t takes the burst approach with a loop of three "descending fours" and one ascending group.

Example 8t:

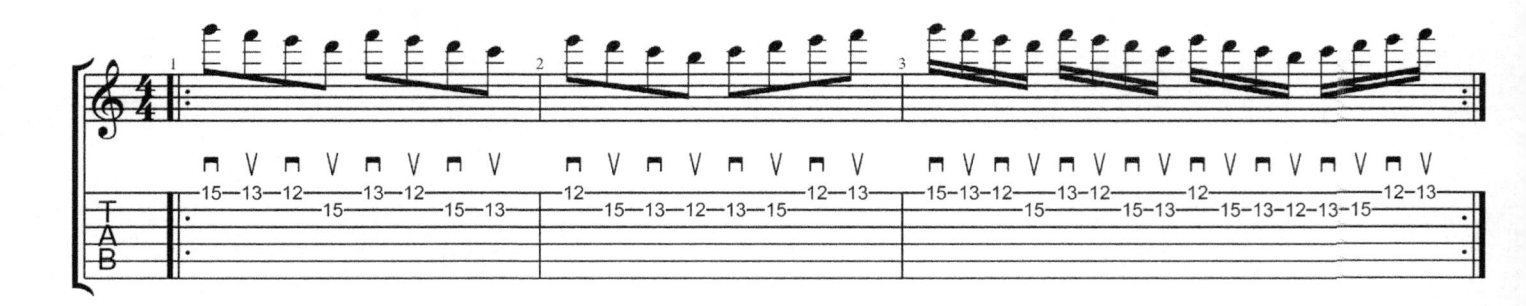

For sweep picking burst practice, Example 8u uses an F major triad with an added B note on the high E string and a D note on the G string (both on the 7th fret).

Example 8u:

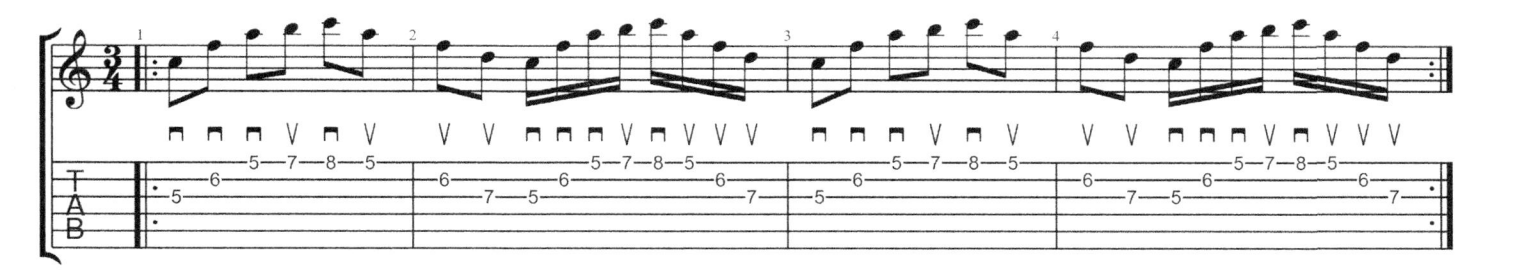

Subdivision bursts are something I use for a more subtle speed increase than the double-speed burst.

Repetition patterns are played in rhythmic groups of four, then accelerated to groups of six. In Example 8v, a six-note pattern is played twice across beats 1, 2, and 3, before beat 4 is played in sextuplets.

A sextuplet burst in this scenario represents a fifty per cent speed increase, so it's a great way to challenge your continuous top speed.

Example 8v:

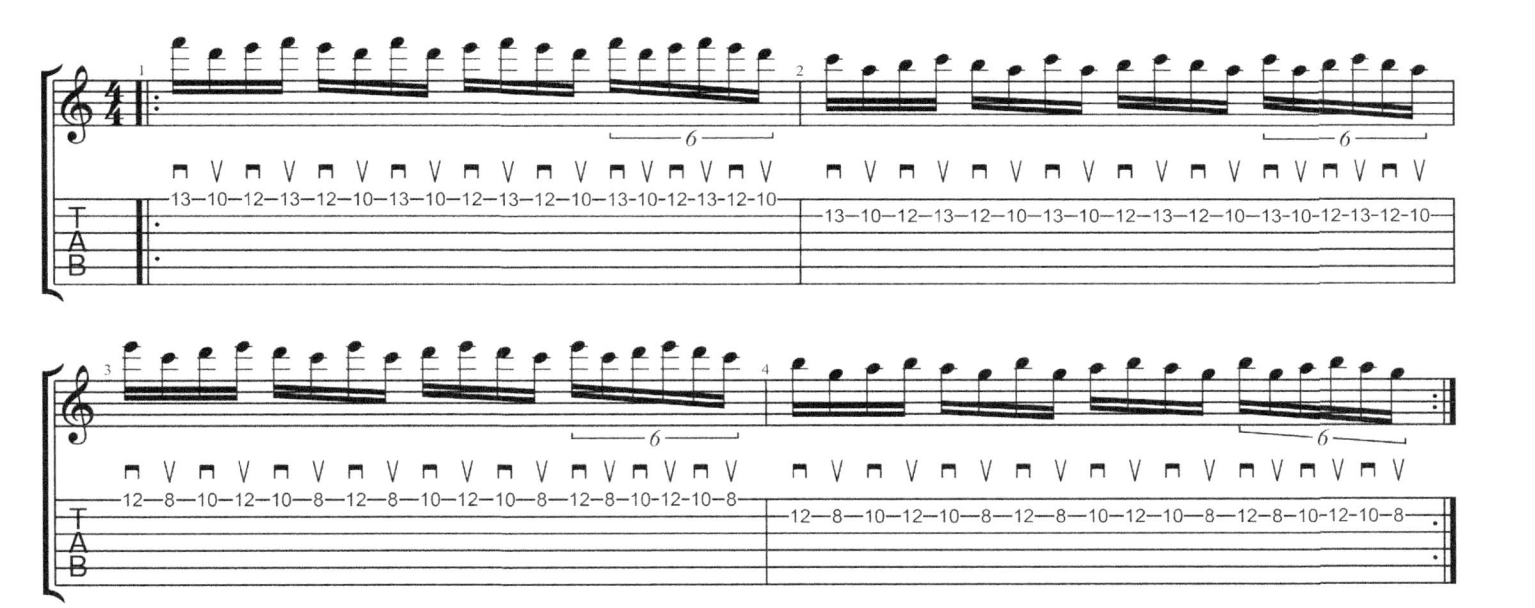

In examples 8w and 8x, the two subdivisions occur in equal amounts. Since the sextuplets take fewer beats to complete than the 1/16th note versions, the bars alternate between 3/4 and 2/4 time.

Example 8w is an alternate picking "ascending fours" pattern, while Example 8x uses economy picking to go up an A minor 7th arpeggio and down the scale.

Example 8w:

Example 8x:

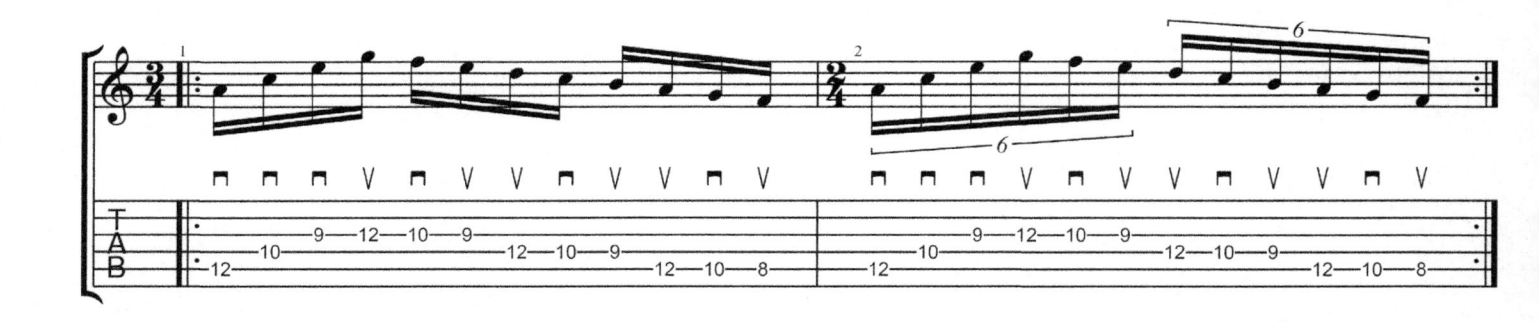

The Science of Modified Practice

Modifying practice drills, which we've done many times in the book, is not just to get you playing on different strings or to make things more interesting. There's actually some science behind using variations and permutations to improve your technique.

According to a study carried out by researchers for the John Hopkins University School of Medicine, altering tasks during repetition-based practice sessions may reduce the time required to master a skill compared to repeating it the same way every time.

In the study, eighty-six volunteers were assigned a computer-based motor skill to learn. The participants who used a modified practice routine performed better in the second test than in the first.

The results supported the notion of reconsolidation, where memories are recalled and augmented with new information to improve motor skills.

According to the study's senior author, Dr Pablo Celnik,

"What we found is if you practice a slightly modified version of a task you want to master, you learn more and faster than if you just keep practicing the same thing multiple times in a row."

"Our results are important because little was known before about how reconsolidation works in relation to motor skill development. This shows how simple manipulations during training can lead to more rapid and larger motor skill gains because of reconsolidation," says Celnik.

"The goal is to develop novel behavioural interventions and training schedules that give people more improvement for the same amount of practice time."

(Source: *Current Biology* journal, January 28, 2016).

To create better, more effective practice routines from the material in this book, and every area you work on, consider reducing the number of tasks you assign yourself in one session, but increase the number of variations used in a practice session.

Three drills and three variations of each are more likely to yield lasting results faster than nine or ten drills repeated the same way each time.

See what new information you can add to drills using the LIE concept, permutations, and the speed practice system outlined in this chapter.

In the next chapter, I'll teach you some of my favourite speed licks to put it all together and increase your endurance.

Chapter Nine: Speed and Endurance Etudes

Maintaining fast playing across longer phrases is the result of speed, synchronization, and sustainable playing habits coming together.

These final drills are designed to apply your hard work to musical phrases and give you some tempo goals.

These four-bar licks have a note density reminiscent of Al Di Meola, Paul Gilbert, and John Petrucci. Even if that's not the ballpark you play in stylistically, it's still great practice for speed, just as violinists use excerpts from Kreutzer and Paganini to hone their chops.

The audio download includes backing tracks at two speeds for each of these examples. Like the other tracks, I call out the tempo at the start of each run-through.

Example 9a includes the sextuplet burst concept from Chapter Eight. Bars one and three use the same melodic motif in different positions, while bars two and four use the reverse sequence in their respective positions.

Example 9a:

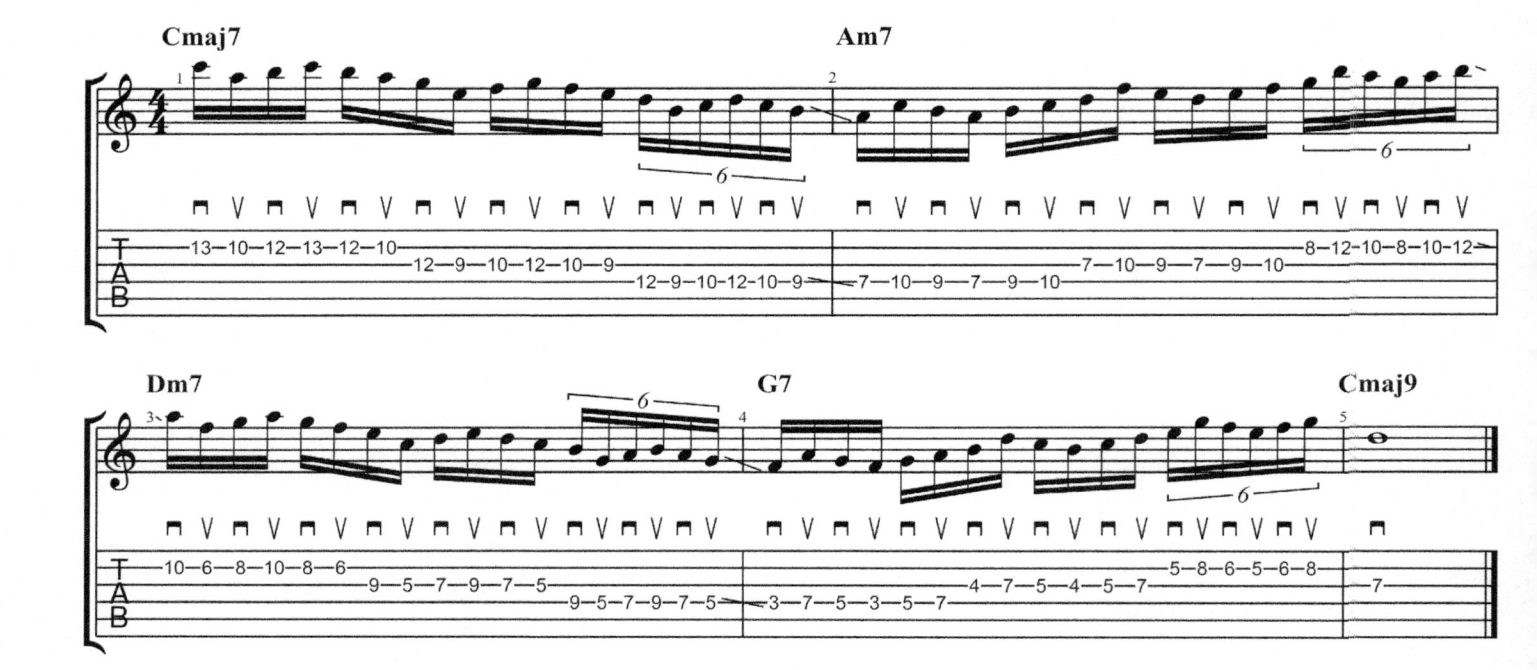

Played over a static F chord for an F Lydian sound, Example 9b uses subdivisions and string skipping to apply exaggerations for both musical and mechanical variety.

I use strong muting on the audio to create dynamic variation in the spots indicated. You can follow the notated playing directions or pick it loud and proud all the way through.

Example 9b:

Bringing some pedal-point to the proceedings, Example 9c is built on a four-note motif in which the highest note of each portion is repeated between the other notes.

The phrase over the E chord in bars one and two borrows F# and G# notes from the A Melodic Minor scale (A B C D E F# G#), and just the G# note from the A Harmonic Minor scale in bar four.

Pedal-tone licks can be very good for endurance, especially when using the pinkie finger as often as this.

Example 9c:

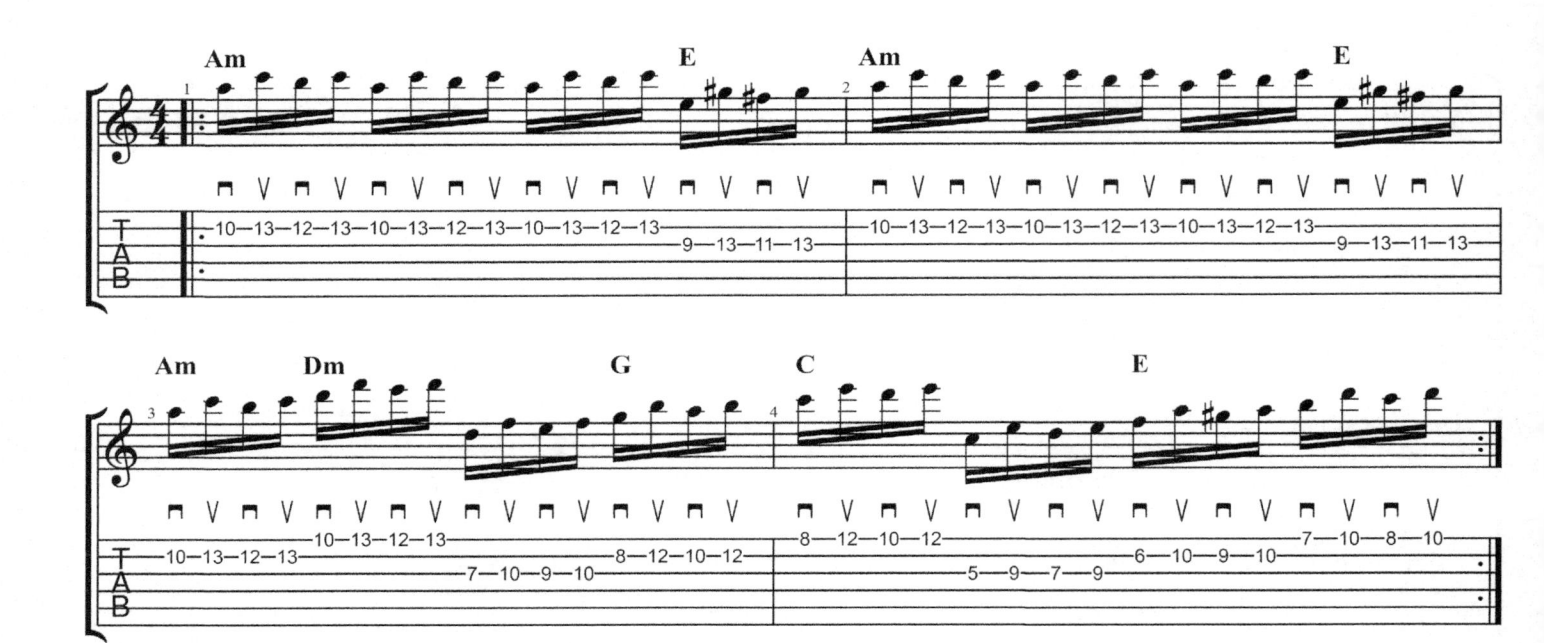

Example 9d contains a motif of eight notes: two notes on the first string of each group and six notes on the string below.

In two-beat intervals, the motif moves around to suit the chord underneath.

Check the fingering that starts each new iteration to ensure you're in the best place to complete each phrase.

Example 9d:

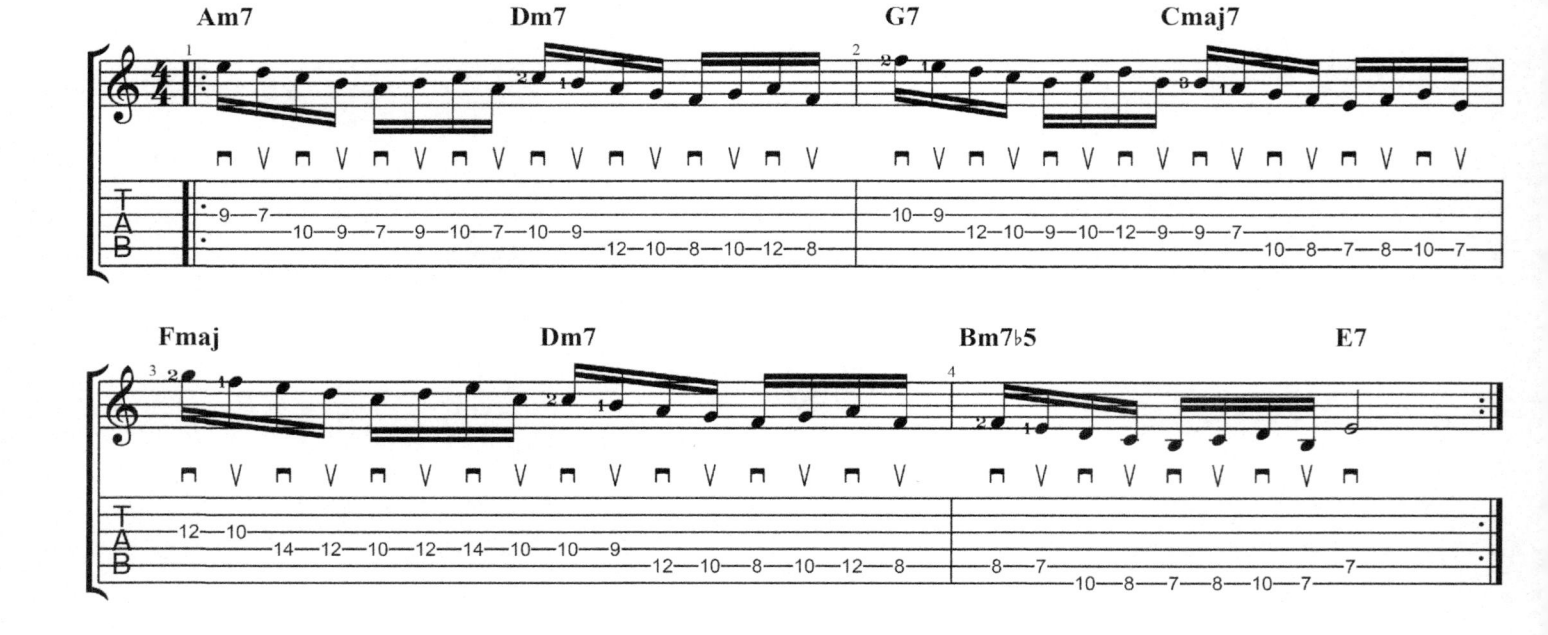

Turning up the heat, bars one, two, and four of the next drill contain note groupings of fourteen. The fourteen notes can be thought of as eight-note, and six-note ideas joined together but, rhythmically, each group is played in the space of sixteen 1/32nd notes.

To develop a time-feel for the groups of fourteen, begin by learning bar one in free time. Then, tap your foot on beats 1 and 3 as you repeat it with even pick strokes. This teaches your brain how each group interacts with two beats of the bar.

Many top shredders have developed this feel for cramming unusual numbers of notes into bars without sounding awkward or uneven. If you play anything with confidence, you can make it work!

Pick strokes are omitted for this example. To work on outside alternate picking string changes, begin with a downstroke and stay with alternate picking throughout.

To work on inside picking string changes, begin with an upstroke.

Example 9e:

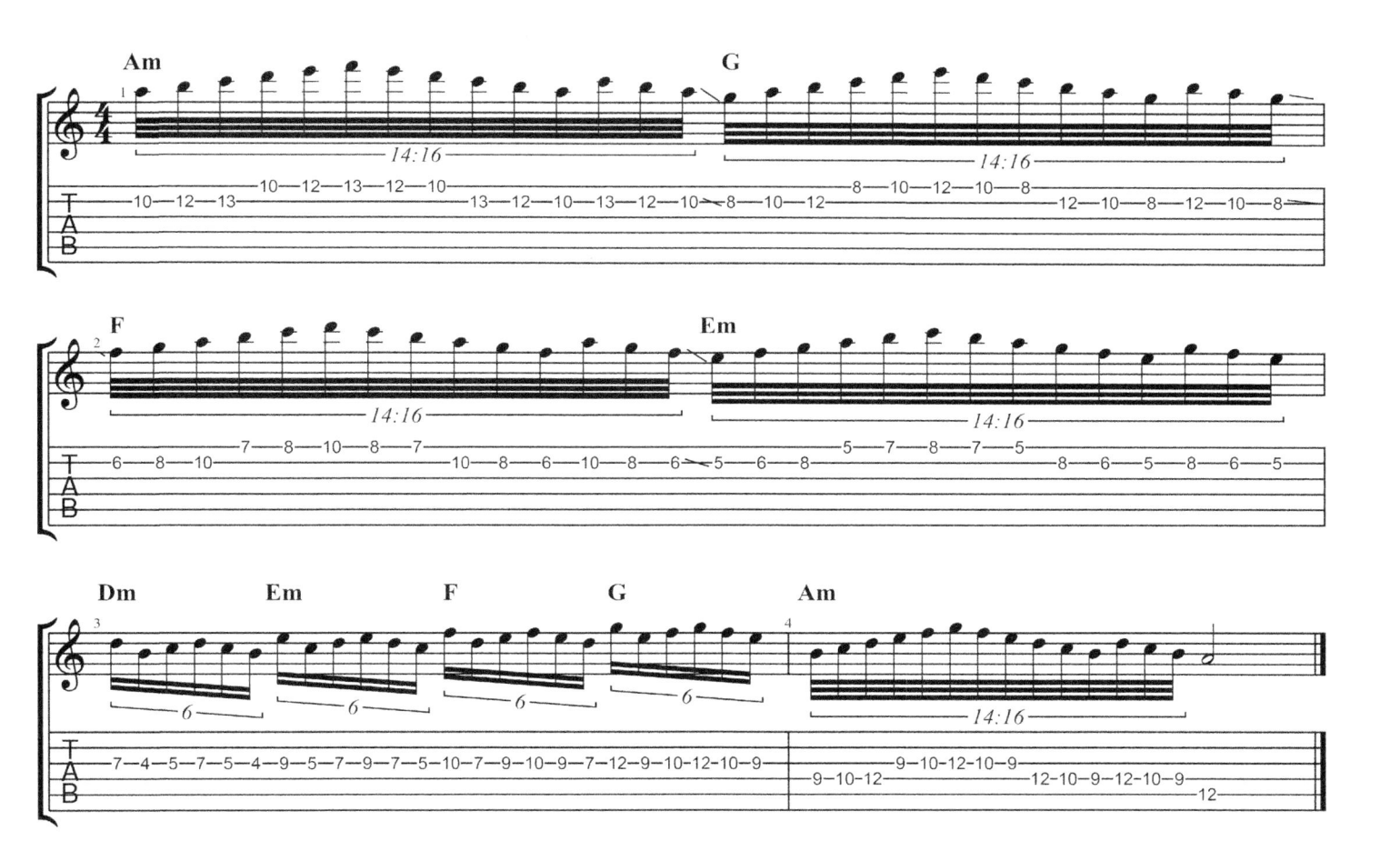

Playing 1/16th notes in melodic groups of ten is pretty uncommon, but this lick is a ripping shred line that calls upon four-note-per-string scales, which also aren't that common.

Focus on the first ten notes in bar one, memorising the sequence of notes and executing the position slide with good timing.

Look through the rest of the lick when you have committed the phrase to memory. You'll see that the phrase is reiterated all over the place but changed to stay within the key.

With a half-time feel on the drums in the backing track, the line comes across as 1/32nd notes, to great effect!

Example 9f:

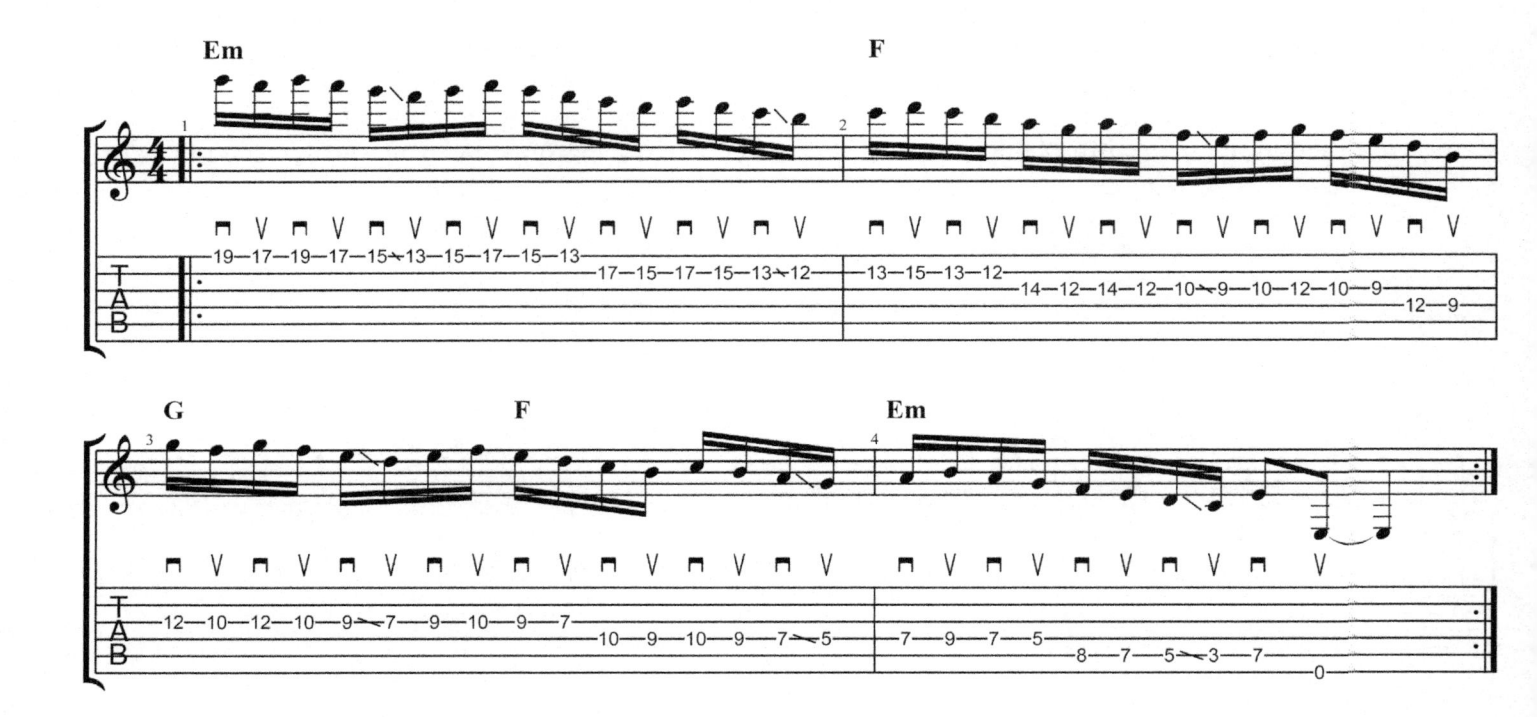

```
Em                                              F
|-19-17-19-17-15-13-15-17-15-13-----------------|-13-15-13-12-----------------------------------|
|-----------------------17-15-17-15-13-12-------|-------------14-12-14-12-10-9-10-12-10-9-------|
|-----------------------------------------------|-------------------------------------------12-9|

G                                               Em
|-12-10-12-10-9-7-9-10-9-7----------------------|-7-9-7-5---------------------------------------|
|-----------------10-9-10-9-7-5-----------------|---------8-7-5-3-7-----------------------------|
|-----------------------------------------------|-------------------0---------------------------|
```

To end with a ripper, Example 9g features a barrage of sextuplet groups reminiscent of Paul Gilbert.

Begin with an upstroke to work on outside picking or a downstroke for inside picking and continue with strict alternate picking from there.

Example 9g:

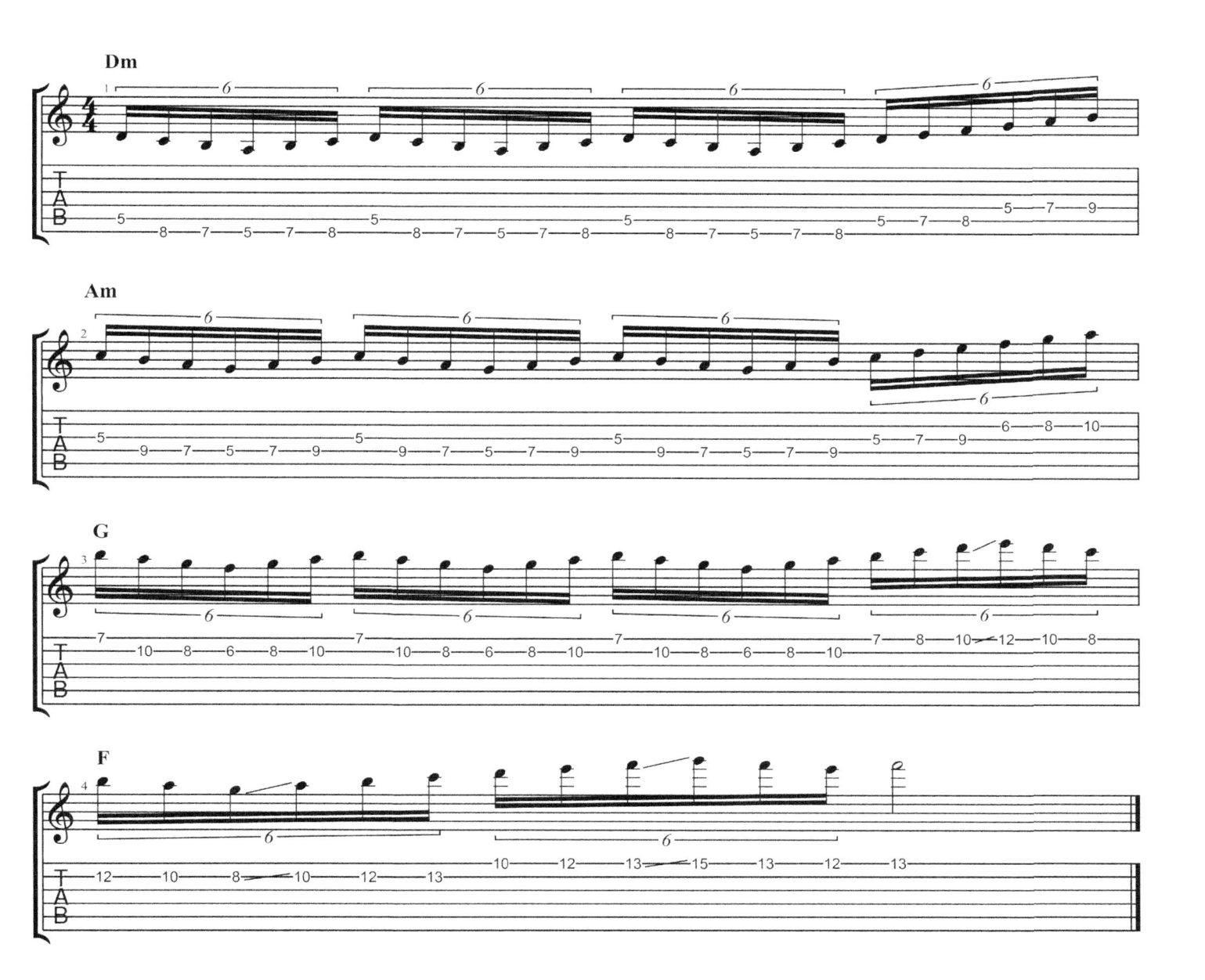

If any aspects of the licks in this chapter were stumbling blocks, i.e., harder than the rest of the lick, see if you can isolate the problem, look for similar drills earlier in the book, or use the speed practice system in Chapter Eight to iron out the problem with interval training.

Section Two Summary

Let's take a quick review of everything covered in this section. Using chapters seven, eight, and nine, you now have processes for:

- Setting up ergonomic posture and guitar positioning
- Minimising fretting hand pressure
- Reducing tension in the picking hand
- Improving pressure independence in the hands
- Compacting information into chunks for your brain to process faster
- Determining your current top speed of a lick
- Reconfiguring drills to practice in bursts
- Practicing in a new way with the metronome
- Establishing new top speeds using interval training
- Playing longer speed lines for endurance

As you revise the chapters in this section, develop a mindset for speed, applying habits, practice routines, and analytics to your daily regimen.

Treat speed as a subject in your practice rather than merely a by-product!

Conclusion

I hope you've found this book a great resource and how-to guide for improving your synchronization and speed.

There's enough material to keep you busy for a long time, so be sure to work through it methodically.

I encourage you to make notes about what needs to be improved in your playing, then come up with a solution. What are the weaknesses? Do you notice a theme to the stumbling blocks?

Try making a list with three columns labelled *Problem*, *Cause*, and *Solution*. It's a process I've found helpful in making breakthroughs happen.

For example, your list might read:

Problem	**Cause**	**Solution**
The third and fourth fingers move together all the time	Not enough independence	Work on the 24 Permutations in Chapter Two
Tension in picking hand	Pick grip is too tight	Revise grip and maintain firm but not tense pressure
Tripping over on string changes	Outside picking is rushed and sloppy	Use the LIE approach to isolate and exaggerate the string change with repeats or string skipping
I can't get a lick up to tempo	I keep practicing at a medium tempo	Come up with an "interval" version of the lick and work on it at higher speeds

When you take a solutions-based approach to everything, you might be able to achieve anything.

Using the tools you've developed in this book, put other players under the microscope. Look at the musical lines, break off chunks of their solos and turn them into drills or etudes.

Multiply the ideas that work great in your technique with as many musical applications as possible. Transpose your best licks to various keys and modes. Create a catalogue of your own licks and use them in real music to reinforce their practicality.

Thanks for trusting me to be your guide. I hope this book has played a part in making you a better player!

Chris.

Other Books by Chris Brooks

100 Arpeggio Licks for Shred Guitar

Advanced Arpeggio Soloing for Guitar

Alternate Picking Guitar Technique

3 in 1 Picking & Tapping Guitar Technique Collection

Economy Picking Guitar Technique

Legato Guitar Technique Mastery

Neo-Classical Speed Strategies for Guitar

Rock Guitar Tapping Technique

Sweep Picking Speed Strategies for Guitar

Sweep Picking Speed Strategies For 7-String Guitar

The Complete Guitar Technique Speed Strategies Collection

Printed in Great Britain
by Amazon